*The* **YEAST-FREE** *Kitchen*

# The YEAST-FREE Kitchen

*Recipes to help you achieve victory over the Yeast-Beast,* **Candida Albicans**

Jane Remington

ISBN: 978-1-365-09841-3

Photographs by Bill Remington
_____

This book is intended to be helpful and educational and is not
intended to replace medical advice or treatment.
_____

This book is dedicated to all seekers of health and wholeness whose search has led them to my cookbook. Your willingness to learn and openness to change will serve you well as you embark on this remarkable journey of self-healing. You will soon be rewarded with victory over Candida albicans.

*Welcome!*

*Author's home in Virginia*

# ACKNOWLEDGMENTS

Loving thanks to my husband, Bill, for your unending support and advice in helping me bring this project into reality. You will always have my heart. And Mamahugs to our children, Craig, Laura, and Mary for your good-natured patience and tolerance during this obsession of so many years.

Special thanks also to the wonderful professionals at Publish Whole-sale, and Mary McCarty in particular, who so skillfully led this novice through the often scary maze of self-publishing.

Huge hugs also to my wonderful son-in-law, Chris Boerboom, for stepping up to the plate and offering your expertise every time my computer went berserk. I'll be forever grateful.

And lastly, my heart-felt thanks to my angel-in-waiting, Linda Berry, who worked so hard to design and format my cookbook to such a beautiful finished product. You were truly heaven-sent!

*Hippocrates, the Father of Medicine*

# PREFACE

Dear Readers,

Now that my book, Recaging the Beast, which explores the yeast/fungal connection to disease, has been published, it is time to expand and update its companion book, The Yeast-Free Kitchen. Since its last publish date of 2004, much more has been learned about yeast and fungi, how they grow, and how and why they produce symptoms and illnesses. The link of fungal overgrowths in the body to disease is now becoming irrefutable.

Also we have learned more about the role diet plays in vanquishing the yeast/beast and speeding up the healing process. It has become abundantly clear that what we put into our mouths can either harm us—or heal us. Getting well has everything to do with the choices we make in the grocery store, in our kitchens, and at out tables.

Unfortunately in the interim years our food supply has been further degraded by the unconscionable addition of GMOs, more antibiotics, stronger herbicides and pesticides, and synthetic chemicals. Our food is fast becoming lethal, and the ever-widening demand for organic fruits, vegetables and meats, and humanely treated animals is reflecting our growing knowledge and understanding of just what makes us healthy—and what makes us sick.

Many of my original recipes will reflect this new level of consciousness, as I have removed some ingredients we have learned can be improved upon, and added more healthful substitutions which have recently become available. In this new edition I have added over 50 new dishes for you to try. All have received thumbs up from family and friends.

I hope you enjoy these recipes. I am always converting, adapting, and experimenting with recipes to make them more healthful—and of course—yeast-free. The health benefits to me and my family (and my family of readers) have been incalculable.

I know they will be for you and yours, too!

Jane Remington
Gordonsville, VA
Spring, 2016

# CONTENTS

*The author's Yeast Free Kitchen*

# INTRODUCTION

## Our Twentieth Century Drama and the Bad Actors of Drugs and Diet

*"The doctor of the future will give no medicine but will interest his patients in the care of the human frame, in diet and prevention of disease."*

—THOMAS EDISON

I f you have been medically diagnosed as having a condition called Candida albicans, or yeast infection, or suspect that you are a "candida candidate," add your name to the list of at least 80 percent of the population of the United States. Misery must love company.

My name was added to that list after I took several courses of antibiotics following gum surgeries thirty years ago. Even though I knew to take acidophilus while taking antibiotics, I didn't take them long enough, and at that time I knew nothing of the yeast-free diet. I developed chronic, systemic candidiasis as a result.

Through a series of events which led me to a remarkable naturopathic physician, I found the yeast-free diet. This diet and holistic approach enabled me to heal myself. It was a miraculous turnaround. During the years since, I have learned everything I could about this tiny microbe, and transformed my cooking and eating so as not to accommodate it!

This normally benign parasite, which lives in the warm, moist recesses of our bodies, has been stimulated to grow out of the normal confines of our digestive tract and now is luxuriating all over our bodies. The first bad actor and prime stimulus to this growth is mainly our twentieth century "wonder drugs"—antibiotics, hormones, steroids and birth control pills. Chronic, systemic candidiasis was almost un-heard of and rarely reported before their advent.

In a nutshell, yeast is a micro-organism which lives everywhere —in the air, on the surface of all living things, living in harmony with other bacteria, fungi, parasites, molds, etc. It is part of the natural order of things. We don't understand its total role inside our bodies, but we do know it was meant to stay mainly in our intestines and wait there until our death. At that time it is programmed to start proliferating and growing all over our bodies with the express purpose of consuming and recycling those bodies back into the earth. *It's main job is to break-down and decompose.* We should be grateful for the role yeast plays in keeping our planet clean and tidy. Otherwise we would all be taking running leaps over dead dinosaurs and sloshing around in the remains of everything that ever lived!

After World War II, as antibiotics, steroids, hormones and birth control pills were introduced, the normal numbers of yeast were stimulated by them to begin growing—prematurely. Yeast then began to break out of its normal confines, reach the bloodstream and lymph channels where it was never intended to go, and circulate throughout the body, hopping out and living on and in the heart, lungs, pancreas, kidneys, ovaries, prostate, brain— any and all tissue—consuming them all for food. The end result, unfortunately, is that we now are being eaten alive. The yeast-beast has learned to live on *living* tissue rather than dead tissue, and now, instead of waiting until we die, the yeast is trying to *decompose us while we are still living.*

You don't have to be a rocket scientist to figure out this can't be good for us! Yeast and their toxins directly invade tissue, and yeast and the poisons they produce can adversely affect all our organ and body systems, interfering with how they function and perform. Yeast toxins literally *disarm* our immune system defenses. In addition, they block hormones and neurotransmitters, all causing a bewildering array of symptoms. As a consequence, Candida albicans is possibly the least understood and most widespread cause of illness in our country today.

The second bad actor in this little drama is diet. In order to survive, yeast must eat. Unfortunately, our Standard American Diet, (or SAD for short), fills the bill of exactly what yeast needs—sugar, milk products, yeast breads, caffeine, alcohol, vinegar and tons of junk food. We can't seem to feed them fast enough. And we are beginning to suspect that yeast and their toxins are what is behind many if not most illnesses, symptoms and diseases. It seems that we have sown the winds of drugs and faulty diet and are now reaping the whirlwind of illness and disease.

The only way to rid the body of excess yeast overgrowths is to take away the yeast's food supply. On average this takes three months of cooking and eating from the "yeast-free diet" to accomplish. If you don't eat what they eat, they starve to death. It's that simple. As yeast levels fall, immune systems are restored, and symptoms and illnesses fade away as organs and body systems begin functioning again, freed from the colonies of yeasts which have been feeding on them. Energy returns in leaps and bounds, physical and mental functioning return to normal, weight normalizes, and in general, life is perceived through new eyes.

For the past thirty years I have worked with hundreds of my naturopath's patients, serving as a guide and consultant to them as they worked their way through the months of healing. I put The Yeast-Free Kitchen together to help make their journey to wholeness easier, first selling it to clients, and then in health food stores. Once I posted it at Amazon, it began spreading its little wings.

It has been an incredibly rewarding experience for me, as I have been witness to more miracles then I can count—all of which are attributable mainly to this diet.

Actually they aren't miracles at all. Miracles are unusual happenings which seem to go against natural law. True healing occurs only when God's natural laws are followed, so the healings which occur around this diet are neither unusual nor unnatural, but both usual and natural!

In any case, I hope you will want to add your name to the list of "miracles" as mine was. It will require resolve, commitment, perseverance, discipline and patience, but you are worth it. Your life and your health are worth it. Your future may depend upon it.

Now, go get well.

Jane Remington

*The author, Jane Remington, editing The Yeast Free Kitchen*

CHAPTER 1

# Symptoms of Yeast Overgrowth

There are direct and indirect correlations of yeast overgrowth to the following list of conditions and diseases:

depression and fatigue

anxiety and panic attacks

gas and bloating

muscle and joint pain

irritability and mood swings

heartburn and acid indigestion

sleep disturbances

constipation and/or diarrhea

"spaciness", dizziness and brain fog

rectal itching, burning, tingling

hallucinations and hearing "voices"

headaches, all kinds

"leaky gut" syndrome

water retention or edema

hyperactivity, ADD and ADHD

poor memory or memory loss

suicidal thoughts

poor concentration

poor coordination

poor circulation

acne and skin rashes

eczema and psoriasis

alcoholism

athlete's foot, jock itch and
    nail fungus

hypoglycemia

asthma and bronchial infections

diabetes

allergies

drug addiction

recurring sinus, ear, nose and
    mouth infections

high cholesterol

weight loss or gain

aching all over

thyroid dysfunction

sore throat

recurring vaginal yeast infections

tinnitus

recurring urinary tract infections

canker sores

hormone imbalances

deafness

chronic stuffy nose and post
  nasal drip

obesity

mitral valve prolapse

insomnia

congestive heart failure

constant hunger

excessive underarm perspiration
  and body odor

sugar cravings

high blood pressure

lupus

"PMS" and menstrual cramps

hiatal hernia

erratic menstrual cycles

diaper rash

endometriosis and infertility

colic

prostatitis and cystitis

impotence

fibroid tumors and fibrocystic breast
disease

eating disorders

miscarriages and birth defects

manic depression

arthritis and rheumatoid arthritis

anemia

numbness and tingling

chest tightness

chronic fatigue syndrome

autism

periodontal disease

cancer (cancer cells are sugar junkies)

And this is only the short list! Please bear in mind that all the symptoms listed here can be caused by conditions other than yeast overgrowth, such as nutritional deficiencies, parasites, some hereditary or congenital conditions, etc. The only way to know for sure what is behind your physical or mental problems is to give the diet a "therapeutic trial." You will know shortly if you are on the right track.

One of the best clues that you are on the right track is called a "healing crisis," or Herxheimer reaction. Soon after you start the diet you may experience headaches, muscle aches and pains, soreness and generalized flu-like symptoms in varying degrees of intensity. This is *Good*! It simply means the yeast are beginning to die and their dead cells and toxins are being dumped into the bloodstream to be eliminated—hence the headaches, aches and pains. The symptoms usually last a few days and then fade away. Stay on the diet and keep going. Several weeks down the road you may break out in a rash, or acne, as yeast toxins are dumped from the liver and eliminated through the skin. This too shall pass. It takes at least three months to catch all the yeast cycles as they start to grow, so as long as you adhere to the diet and don't feed new crops, they will eventually die.

Don't forget that chronic candidiasis is not just an annoyance, or a simple, benign condition. It can be lethal. As yeast and its toxins destroy the immune system, you then become susceptible to major, life-threatening disease.

If you already have serious illness, such as cancer or heart disease, are obese, or have severe mental problems, please commit to the diet for six months to a year. Healing from candida is like peeling the layers of an onion. Some yeast burrow very deeply into tissue, and it may take many months to get to the deepest pockets. This is especially true of the brain.

Many of you are familiar with other versions of the yeast-free diet. Some are much more restrictive than this one, not allowing any fruits the first month, restricting barley malt, grains, peanuts, flavoring extracts, or severely limiting carbohydrates such as corn and potatoes. Most of these restrictions are not necessary, and severely restricting carbohydrates can shock the pancreas and adrenal glands. It is best to eat them moderately in order for the body to have time to adjust. Other versions incorrectly allow things which *should not* be eaten, such as beef and pork, yogurt and bananas. No wonder it takes a year or more on those diets to get rid of yeast overgrowth. This is the diet which works the quickest and the best, so please follow directions carefully.

As you finish the diet, please ease off slowly. Don't run out the first day and eat pizza and drink beer. You will undo a lot of good. Try a piece of yeast toast the first day, then stay on the diet for the rest of the day. The second day, try half of a banana, and a cookie and hop back on the diet for the day. If you have no adverse reactions, such as cramps, diarrhea, headache, etc., keep easing off very gently.

To me the most beautiful part of this diet (it's not a "di-et" but actually a "die-off"), is that you will not want to go back to eating the Standard American Diet. SAD will not appeal to you very much. The yeast themselves, which set up the cravings for alcohol, sugar, yeast breads, vinegar, chocolate, caffeine and milk products will be gone, and you will both want to eat and enjoy what is good for you. You will truly be transformed.

Tell someone you love.

CHAPTER II

# The Diet (not as bad as it looks!)

*"I will take the blood from their mouths, the forbidden food from between their teeth."*

—ZECHARIAH 9:7

## Do NOT Eat or Drink:

**Alcohol**   beer, wine, or anything fermented. All alcohols are fermented. Anything femented contains yeast. Alcohol is really the mycotoxin (yeast poison) made by yeast.

**Coffee**   decaf, tea, or anything containing caffeine. Caffeine is a stimulant, and will stimulate the growth of yeast. Even decaf will stimulate yeast, is acidic and also addictive.*

**Sugar**   or artificial sweeteners of any kind, including fructose, maltose, lactose, sucrose, cane sugar, agave syrup, galactose, molasses, date sugar, maple sugar, turbinado sugar, Aspartame, Nutra-sweet, Equal or Splenda (yeasts' favorite food)**

**Bread**   containing yeast, including pita bread and most crackers

**Milk**   and milk products of all kinds, including yogurt, cheese, cottage cheese, ice cream, buttermilk, sour cream, cream cheese (they contain the milk sugar lactose which feeds yeast.

| | |
|---|---|
| **Beef** | veal or pork (contain steroids, hormones, myc toxins and antibiotics) Also highly acidic and yeast thrives in acid. |
| **Some Fruits** | grapes, bananas, plums, raisins, and all dried fruits, including prunes (Bananas are the highest "sugar fruit" on earth. The touches of white you see on grapes, plums and dried fruits are colonies of yeast.) |
| **Condiments** | such as ketchup, commercial mayonnaise, teriyaki, tabasco, mustard, Worcestershire sauce, barbecue sauces, soy sauce, tamari, miso—all contain sugar and vinegar. |
| **Oils** | safflower, corn, soybean, peanut, and canola oils. All are omega 6 oils which create inflammation in the body. Also, most are genetically modified now, making them even more dangerous. |
| **Mushrooms** | All are the fruiting bodies of yeast and fungi. We are trying to *rid* the body of yeast and fungi. They grow in doo-doo in the dark. No chlorophyll, no sunshine. Yuck. Why would an one want to eat them? Also, all mushrooms feed the fungal population in the gut, they disrupt the intestinal flora and are also loaded with glutamate, a known cancer fertilizer! Despite all the hype about medicinal mushroom, there is no such thing as a good mushroom. |
| **Margarine** | pickles or green olives (Margarine contains hydrogenated oils, pickles and olives are swiming in vinegar and are indigestible.) |
| **Preservatives** | M.S.G., hydrolyzed protein, artificial colors or dyes (Yeast loves to munch on that stuff.) |
| **Vinegar** | of all kinds, or sauerkraut (Because of fermentation they contain mold.) |
| **Chocolate** | (sugar and caffeine) |
| **Yeast** | (self-explanatory) |
| **Yeast Extracts** | (self-explanatory) |

| | |
|---|---|
| **Brewers Yeast** | (self-explanatory) |
| **Soft Drinks** | full of sugars and dyes—also the phosphates in soft drinks push calcium out of the bloodstream, literally creating soft bones. ***Remember, soft drinks mean soft bones*** \*\*\* |
| **Canned** | vegetables and fruits in general, with the exception of canned tomatoes, tomato sauce, tomato paste, chilies, water chestnuts |
| **Antibiotics** | birth control pills, prescription drugs, steroids, and hormones should be avoided unless your physician finds them absolutely necessary. |
| **Frozen Dinners** | cheap ingredients, loaded with salt. |
| **Packaged Food** | cheap ingredients, loaded with salt. |
| **Fast Food** | No one who made them loves you! |

\*We have learned so much in recent years of the harmful effects of caffeine that I want to pass on to you some of the latest findings. Caffeine is now the #1 drug of choice in this country. Coffee and soft drinks are the delivery systems of choice, but caffeine is also found in tea, cocoa, medications and chocolate. As few as one to two cups (100 - 300 mg) a day can cause damage throughout the body as it throws body chemistry out of balance. It is clearly addictive and contributes to palpitations, sleeplessness, panic attacks, hypoglycemia, PMS, fatigue, cardiovascular disease, depression, gastrointestinal disease, fibrocystic breast disease, anemia, fibromyalgia, migraines, cancer, hypertension and more. Because caffeine affects the body's ability to absorb calcium, osteoporosis is now rampant.

Of all the consumable foods on earth, coffee beans are the most heavily sprayed with chemical pesticides, herbicides and fungicides. Caffeine is a psychoactive (mood altering) drug which is chemically related to morphine, nicotine and cocaine—all of which are poisonous. Caffeine harms all organs, but profoundly stresses the adrenals.

Stressed, exhausted adrenals can lead to autoimmune diseases such as rheumatoid arthritis, lupus, MS, vitiligo and allergies, asthma and chronic fatigue syndrome. No person can be restored to full health until his adrenals are restored to full health too. The best and quickest way to do this is to remove caffeine from the diet.

Caffeine causes an increased loss of B vitamins (our energy vitamins) calcium, magnesium, sodium, chloride, potassium and zinc in the urine. A single cup of coffee (150 mg.) can reduce iron absorption in a single meal by as much as 75%. Is it any wonder that the third most common reason Americans seek medical help is *fatigue.*

Caffeine also suppresses melatonin (which helps us sleep, boosts the immune system and is an anti-anxiety agent) and decreases blood flow and oxygen to the brain. As little as 100 mg. can significantly decrease recall, reasoning and mental acuity. It has been linked to heart arrythmias, mitral valve prolapse, coronary vasospasm and elevated homocysteine levels (a biochemical which damages the linings of blood vessels and leads to blocked arteries) and damages nerve cells. Caffeine is implicated in heartburn, ulcers, and chronic muscle tension, is a trigger for migraines, is dehydrating, accelerates aging (especially of skin and kidneys), damages DNA, depletes hormones and raises blood sugar levels, fatty acid levels and stress hormone levels.

Caffeine has the ability to cross the placenta to the developing baby and has been shown to cause birth defects ranging from cleft palate to missing toes and fetal growth retardation. It is a known factor in miscarriage, premature births, premature rupture of membranes and fetal death. Very recently the prestigious British Medical Journal published a paper showing the relationship of caffeine's toxic effects on fetal development which included damage done to the pancreatic cells that produce insulin—setting the stage for diabetes in later life! This study also found that countries where caffeine consumption was lowest had the lowest incidence of diabetes, and countries which had the highest caffeine consumption had the highest incidence of diabetes.

If you think decaf is the way to go, think again. Most coffee companies use a harsher, cheaper bean (robusta) in their decaffeinated coffees. It contains more acid than regular coffee, causing a higher secretion of stomach acid resulting in acid indigestion and heartburn. Caffeine is extracted from coffee beans (unless the European water method is used) using a solvent called methylene chloride—a known carcinogen. Decaf raises cholesterol higher and faster than regular coffee and still affects blood sugar levels in diabetics. All in all a health-destroying product.

If this thumbnail sketch doesn't convince you to "ban the bean" (or at least severely restrict it) I urge you to read Caffeine Blues listed under recommended reading. It is one of the most intelligent, well-written and well-researched books on the subject to date.

**Aspartame (Nutrasweet, Equal, Candarel, Spoonful, Equal-Measure and Twin Sweet) is now being consumed by half the adult population in the United States. Worldwide consumer action has exposed this artificial sweetener for the deadly poison it is, and with any luck it will be banned in the next few years.

The FDA has received more complaints about this product than any other, as evidence is mounting that it causes or aggravates headaches, seizures, memory loss, neurological disorders, (especially MS) visual problems, tinnitus, diabetic complications, lupus, allergies, depression, bi-polar disorder, dizziness, eating disorders, hypoglycemia, female hair loss, Alzheimer's disease, Parkinson's disease, chronic fatigue syndrome, cancer and many others. The FDA also lists 92 official symptoms including *death.* It is banned in Europe for children's products and in the USA it can be found in over 6,000 foods including OTC medications, chewing gum and children's vitamins.

Aspartame is a deadly neuro (nerve) toxin. If the temperature exceeds 86° F, the methanol (also known as wood alcohol—the poison known to cause blindness and death in "skid row" alcoholics) in aspartame converts to *formaldehyde* (embalming fluid!) and then to formic acid—the poison found in the sting of fire ants! Our Desert Storm troops drank huge amounts of aspartame-sweetened beverages which had been heated to well over 86° F in the hot Saudi Arabian sun. (Could the mysterious neurological symptoms many of our service men and women exhibited after the war be caused by methanol/formaldehyde poisoning?) Aspartame is 10% wood alcohol.

Formaldehyde is grouped in the same class of drugs as cyanide and arsenic—lethal poisons—and was recently found in the retina of the eye. It doesn't kill as quickly as cyanide and arsenic, but quietly takes its time. It is actually more toxic than some narcotic drugs, yet Aspartame remains legal.

Aspartame is made from two amino acids, aspartic acid and phenylalanine, which are found naturally with other amino acids in protein. Aspartame uses aspartic acid and phenylalanine alone, making an unnatural product which becomes neuro-toxic without the missing amino acids. At this point it can pass the blood brain barrier and deteriorate the neurons of the brain. The ingredients can literally stimulate the neurons of the brain to death, causing brain damage of varying degrees and changes to the chemistry of the brain. Phenylalanine breaks down into DKP, a brain tumor agent, and is known to lower the seizure threshold and deplete seratonin, (your calming neurotransmitter), causing seizures, manic depression, panic attacks, rage and violence. Suppressed seratonin levels also create craving for carbohydrates and will make you *fat*! (Formaldehyde is stored in fat cells, particularly in the hips and thighs.) It also alters the dopamine levels, crucial to those suffering from Parkinson's Disease. The wood alcohol (methanol) in Aspartame is deadly to diabetics as it can cause blood sugar levels to go haywire. Methanol toxicity mimics symptoms of MS, Parkinsons and systemic lupus (rampant among Diet Coke and Diet Pepsi drinkers) causing many misdiagnoses. Could this be the reason Michael J. Fox was diagnosed with Parkinson's Disease—an old person's disease—at age 30, after becoming a spokesperson for Pepsi and Diet Pepsi?

Don't be fooled by the new boy on the block, Splenda, either. Even though it is made from sugar, Splenda is produced by *chlorinating* the sugar. (Chlorine is a carcinogen). The structure of the sugar molecule is chemically changed by substituting three chlorine atoms for three hydroxy groups. At this point, studies on rats and rabbits have shown many problems, such as severely shrunken thymus glands, enlarged livers and kidneys, diarrhea, decreased red blood count, etc. Its long-term safety is unknown as *no human research has been done.* There isn't even an established system for monitoring and tracking reported adverse reactions and side effects. It's no wonder most European countries have not approved its use, awaiting further review.

Like caffeine, Aspartame and most artificial sweeteners are addictive, which makes their manufacturers happy. The more people that are hooked, the more money they make. The high-intensity sweetener market is huge—bringing in $1.5 billion a year, and drug and chemical lobbies have very deep pockets. It seems greed and profit come before people's lives and health. Doctors and health professionals everywhere who are educated on this subject are referring to its use as a "plague" causing a "major American health disaster" and a "world epidemic". There are thousands of pages on the web for you to visit and study, such as: www.dorway.com, sweetpoison.com, aspartamekills.com, mercola.com and many others. Please save your life and health and banish this menace from your and your loved ones diets.

***Soft drinks, in my opinion, are the number one contributing factor to the decline in our nation's health. They are so much a part of the fabric of our economic and social culture we can't imagine life without them. Of all the countries of the industrialized west, the United States ranks 24th in overall health, a shocking statistic. Refined sugar, caffeine and artificial sweeteners lead the list of reasons for this decline. *All are found in soft drinks.*

The average teenage boy in this country now drinks 15 teaspoons of sugar in soft drinks every day, and a girl 10 teaspoons. You would gag if you sat down to eat 10 - 15 teaspoons of sugar, but in a soft drink it floats down your throat, creating blood sugar problems, metabolic stress and malnutrition by stimulating the excretion of B vitamins, calcium, copper and chromium. Soft drinks are very high in phosphates (phosphoric acid) which literally push calcium out of the blood stream, and will melt nails and remove rust if you are so inclined. The acidity of a soft drink is about the same as vinegar, which nobody can drink straight. But when a ton of sugar, dyes and flavorings are added to mask the acidity, who's to know!

Soft drinks contain no nutrition, and their use contributes to insufficient intake of calcium, magnesium, riboflavin, vitamin A, and vitamin C. Caffeinated soft drinks have an adverse effect on the absorption and metabolism of the *entire diet* (The soft drink manufacturers buy their caffeine as a by-product from the production of decaf coffee!) Soft drinks are linked to depression, bone fractures, neurological damage, hypertension, and all the symptoms and diseases listed under caffeine and artificial sweeteners.

Today soft drink sales have risen to a mind-boggling fifty-five gallons a year for every man, woman, and child in America. Children are the most vulnerable to the ill- effects of soft drinks as their immature systems (especially their brains and nervous systems) are not fully developed and equipped to metabolize this poison. Early addictions will lead to a lifetime of painful and expensive consequences. Soft drinks are probably the most successfully marketed product since the dawn of man, and the main reason for this success is its *addictive quality.* The next time you are in a school, notice the contract—mandated advertising inside and outside the buildings, on scoreboards, fences, roofs, cups, banners, and vending machines. Money (bribes?) from cola companies fund sports programs, computer programs, athletic scholarships and more, to the delight of schools who see this as easy money. Cola companies are more than delighted to lend a helping hand to the next generation of addicts. As of this writing most soft drink manufacturers are still refusing to put warning labels on their products or disclose amounts of caffeine. Their bottom lines are more important. Just say no.

*"Listen, listen to me and eat what is good, and your soul will delight in the richest of fare."*

ISAIAH 55:2

## You MAY Eat and Drink:

Chicken, fish, turkey, or lamb—preferably organic, not smoked

Venison, bison, and all wild game

Fresh vegetables, preferably organic

Beans, rice, potatoes, pastas in moderation

Grains, such as wheat, oats, rye, barley, millet, amaranth, quinoa (unless allergic) couscous, grits

Citrus fruits, strawberries, kiwi, melons, apples, pears, peaches, raspberries, blackberries, papaya, pineapple

Butter, eggs, rice milk, and rice cheeses

Yeast-free breads, including natural yeast-free sourdough

Tortillas and rice cakes

Tortilla chips and homemade guacamole

Muffins, cornbread, biscuits, pancakes made with almonds or rice milk

Nuts and nut butters such as peanut butter, almond butter, cashew butter, sunbutter, with added vitamin C powder

Honey, maple syrup, rice syrup, barley malt, unsweetened apple butter in moderation

Tofu occasionally, and organic please

Herb teas, especially Taheebo, and unsweetened juices

Mineral, filtered or spring water

Popcorn, (occasionally and organic only), pumpkin seeds, sunflower seeds

Carob powder and unsweetened carob chips

Roma, Pero, Dandy Blend, or Take-a-Break herb tea in place of coffee

Rice Dream Ice Cream (wonderful in milkshakes made with almond or coconut milk

Salads and slaws

Unsweetened applesauce

Oils, such as, extra-virgin olive oil, flax oil, preferably cold-pressed,
   organic coconut oil, nut oilsl

Please supplement the diet daily with tried and true yeast killers to speed healing. Some of the best to choose from are monolaurin, Kyolic garlic capsules, olive leaf extract, caprylic acid, Candida Cleanse, Cand-Aid, Yeast Fighters, grapefruit seed extract, oregano oil, and various homeopathics. Everyone should take an acidophilus-bifidus supplement or a probiotic to help restore the deranged intestinal flora, and digestive enzymes with each meal to help extract the most nutrition from each meal.

One of the most important presents you can give yourself is to drink 2 quarts of pure water every day—for the rest of your life. (Not including juices, coffee, tea, soft drinks because they are all dehydrating.) This will both flush toxins out of your body AND rehydrate your cells—giving huge boosts to your immune system. Also be sure to consume at least ½ tsp. sea salt or seasoned salt daily, especially when increasing water intake. Low salt diets are dangerous and counter-productive, and can lead to osteoporosis, acidosis, muscle cramps and even cancer. The best book to read on this subject is Your Body's Many Cries For Water, by F. Batmanghelidj, M.D. His website is www.watercure.com. It is a very important book. Please read and heed!

After you have healed, look for a wonderful herbal "coffee" called Teeccino. By then you won't want or need anything containing caffeine. (Teeccino can't be allowed on the yeast-free diet since it contains dates and figs.) It is brewed like coffee and is made from herbs, grains, fruits and nuts. It also contains potassium for a natural energy lift, and is alkalizing. My husband and I enjoy it for breakfast with a little coconut creamer and a touch of stevia powder for sweetening, and after dinner it is delicious iced. It comes in Java, Mocha, Almond, Amaretto, Vanilla Nut, Hazelnut and Chocolate Mint.

CHAPTER III

## Eating Yeast-Free

Now we are coming to the good part—looking at what you CAN eat. There's hope! As you can readily see, there is a lot to choose from, and no one is going to starve to death. Shopping in the grocery store will be very simple, quick, and easy since you can't buy ninty-five percent of the stuff!

Begin by cleaning out the refrigerator and cupboards of anything and everything on the "no-no" list. No reason to keep temptation around. Then head for the health food store or your grocery store and stock the kitchen with healing foods.

Normally, my family sticks very closely to the diet most of the time, and every three months we do it strictly for three weeks to make sure our yeast levels remain low. That way, when we eat out or travel we feel free to eat whatever we want, but hop right back on the diet when we get home.

At home you will be modifying your favorite recipes, and most make the transition very well. Have fun and get creative. In recipes that call for mushrooms, eliminate them or substitute water chestnuts. If a recipe calls for bread crumbs, use rolled oats or crushed yeast-free crackers. In recipes calling for milk, use coconut milk, almond or rice milk straight or diluted with water. You can hardly tell the difference.

You will notice that in many of my recipes I use a lot of herbs and spices, most of which have either a suppressing effect on yeast or a cleansing and healing effect on the body. Garlic, cinnamon, turmeric, cumin, ginger, cilantro, garam masala, Herbamare, and horseradish are a few of my favorites.

It may seem expensive at first as you look at the prices of alternative milks in comparison to cow's milk, or organic meats and vegetables, or yeast-free breads and butter. But if you look again at the prices of soft drinks, beer, alcohol, beef, pork, bacon, veal, sugars and sugar-filled cereals, cookies, ice creams, etc., things you WON'T be buying, (hopefully ever again) you may be spending less. On top of that, think of the antibiotics and other drugs you won't have to buy, (hopefully ever again). In every way you will come out ahead.

Several readers have written to me questioning my occasional use of white flour or evaporated cane juice. It is important to remember that ingesting small quantities of questionable foods is actually a good thing. When all "no-no's" are removed from the diet, the immune system is never challenged. When the immune system is never challenged it becomes lazy. When it becomes lazy, soon it will become depleted and won't work at all. Not a good thing. So small occasional challenges can actually work in your favor!

A word about honey and maple syrup. Most yeast-free diets say they are forbidden. But keep in mind that honey and maple syrup are HEALERS. Honey (raw and organic) is loaded with anti-oxidants, vitamins, minerals, and enzymes to nourish the yeast-ravaged body, and maple syrup (pure grade B) contains less fructose than any other syrup. It also has every vitamin, mineral and trace mineral than man is known to need. In my experience, when a small amount of these sweeteners is ingested at the end of a meal which contains protein, the sugars in them are metabolized slowly enough so that blood sugar and yeast levels are not adversely affected.

This diet works slowly and gently, without putting the body into shock through severe restrictions which cause the body to de-tox too rapidly. It is very important to keep you feeling "undeprived" and satisfied during this time. Otherwise you might get bored or frustrated and declare defeat. But please, no more than two to three small servings of desserts a week during the first three weeks, if at all, and thereafter only moderate amounts. Slow and easy wins this race.

In our house, food comes first. All the possessions of life aren't worth having if you aren't well enough to enjoy them. Remember—a family is no healthier than the food that comes out of its kitchen.

### Chicken, Fish, Turkey, and Lamb

Please try to get these organic and fresh, if possible, and not smoked. Canned tuna, salmon, and sardines are okay.

*"Let your food be your medicine and your medicine be your food."*

HIPPOCRATES

### Beans, Pastas, Potatoes, Rices, and Grains

Remember to eat moderate amounts, because of the high carbohydrate counts. Never more than one medium-sized portion of carbohydrate per meal.

### Fresh Vegetables

Organic, if possible. The more vegetables you eat, the better. They contain vitamins and minerals for healing, and chlorophyll for cleansing. Foods from plant sources have natural fungal inhibitors which keep plants from being consumed by the fungi in the soil and air. When we eat them, they naturally inhibit yeast.

### Fruits

Only one or two a day from the acceptable list the first month, preferably for breakfast. A small glass of juice counts as one serving of fruit. Dilute with water the first month.

### Butter

Enjoy. It is made from pure fat and contains very little lactose or milk sugar to feed yeast. Contains vitamins (A, E, K & D) and minerals (selenium and iodine) and essential fatty acids which protect against gastrointestinal infections and is anti- cancer, antimicrobial, and antifungal.

### Eggs

Find organic eggs if possible. They come from chickens which are raised naturally, and are allowed to scratch on real ground for their food. Also they benefit from natural sunlight, and from being around roosters. (Keeps their hormones balanced.) Commercial chickens are raised in unnatural environments, where they live in crowded cages, never see sunlight, are artificially stimulated by artificial light to make them lay more eggs. Their feed is mixed with antibiotics, dyes, hormones, tranquilizers, plus their own *recycled waste.* To add insult to injury, they are fed growth steroids which cause bacteria to proliferate, and *then* they have to be fed antibiotics to control the bacteria!

### Rice, Almond, Coconut, Hemp Milks

There are many wonderful and delicious alternative milks on the market now. Soymilk is now almost 90% genetically modified so I no longer recommend it. Almond milk, rice milk, coconut milk, and hemp milk are delicious and can be substituted in all recipes calling for milk. Some make Lite lines if you want to cut calories

### Yeast-Free Breads

They are out there, and most are delicious. Some sourdoughs are acceptable if there is no added yeast or milk. Our favorite is an organic yeast-free bread by Monterey. Most tortillas are yeast-free, but read labels carefully. I always toast them lightly, butter them, and add a sprinkle of sea salt. Rice cakes can be used for bread in a pinch.

### Nuts and Nut Butters

Some of the other versions of the yeast-free diet restrict peanuts, and peanut butter, if not all nuts, because of their tendency to mold. All I can say is that most of the people I have worked with eat nuts and nut butters in moderation, and get well anyway, so I don't see any reason to eliminate them, unless allergic. I do suggest that you get fresh ground, add ¼ tsp. powdered vitamin C and refrigerate immediately. Try cashew butter, almond butter, or sunflower butter for a change.

### Honey, Maple Syrup, Rice Syrup, Unsweetened Apple Butter

Moderate, occasional amounts won't hurt. Refrigerate maple syrup (grade B is best) and any unsweetened jams or fruit butters and add ¼ tsp. of powdered vitamin C to each jar to suppress and neutralize any mold.

### Baking Powder Breads, Pancakes, and Waffles

Muffins, biscuits, cornbread, pancakes, and waffles can all be made using half water and half soymilk for the milk. Most recipes are easy to convert and taste very good. Use only aluminum-free baking powder. I use Rumford's.

### Beverages

Pero, Dandy Blend, and Roma are delicious coffee substitutes, as is Take A Break Herb Tea, by Bigelow. Herb teas are fine, and occasional fruit juices diluted by half with water are acceptable. Drink filtered or spring water only, to keep chlorine, fluoride, and other additives out of your body. Perrier and other natural mineral waters with fresh lemon or lime are delicious.

If you do buy juices, please read labels like a hawk. The front label may say "l00 natural, no sugar added", and when you read the list of ingredients you may find the sweetener is concentrated grape juice—a big no-no, since grapes are forbidden. Always dilute fruit juices with water to cut the sugar content.

### Condiments

Mayonnaise, mustard and ketchup must be homemade. Check my recipes.

### Snacks

Occasional organic popcorn, roasted and salted pumpkin seeds, tortilla and corn chips with homemade salsa or guacamole.

### Cheeses

These have to be rice cheeses, of course. They bake especially well. In the third month you may have some feta. Make sure the feta is made of sheep's milk and not cow's.

### Oils

Get organic, extra-virgin and cold pressed if you can. Coconut, flaxseed, nut oils such as walnut, macadamia, and almond, and extra-virgin and light olive are good choices. Vegetable oils such as safflower, corn, soybean and canola are not allowed as they are highly processed, contain inflammatory omega-6 fatty acids, and most are genetically modified these days.

So as you can see there is *plenty* to eat. There is no reason for someone who doesn't need to lose weight to lose weight, and there is every reason for someone who needs to lose weight to do so.

If you are already thin, try to eat five or six times a day. Drink almond milk, eat nuts, potatoes, oils, etc., and you shouldn't lose weight. In an overweight person, as the body balances and the metabolism wakes up, the pounds drop off naturally.

Following is a partial list of foods by brand names you can find in health food stores. Some may even be found in grocery stores. If your stores don't carry them, ask the manager to order them for you. Most are very obliging.

## In Health Food Stores

There are so many different brands to choose from these days. Here are a few of the ones I've found to be acceptable. Most of these products come from Whole Foods. I hope you are lucky enough to have one close by.

### Frozen Foods:

Amy's Vegetable Pie

Amy's Rice & Bean Burritos

Amy's Mexican Tamale Pie

Amy's Breakfast Burritos Amy's Apple Pie

Shelton's Uncured Chicken

Smart Dogs and Turkey Franks

### Ice Creams:

Rice Dream:

Strawberry, Wildberry, Vanilla, Carob Bars—Vanilla dipped in
    Carob Coating

Sweet Nothings: Very Blueberry, Raspberry Swirl

## Rice and Almond Cheeses:

Veggie Parmesan by Soyco

TofuRella

Rice Parmeson by Soyco

Almond Rella

Good Slice

Light 'N' Lean

## Seasonings:

Bragg's Liquid Aminos

Herbamare

Santay Garlic Magic

Trocomare

Bernard Jenson's Natural Vegetable Seasoning and Instant Gravy

De Souza's Solar Sea Salt

Garlic Gomasio

Hain's Chili Seasoning Mix

Adobo Seasoning by Fronteir

Jane's Crazy Mix-Up Salt

## Canned Soups and Foods

Health Valley:

    Black Bean

    Chicken Broth

    Minestrone

Pacific: Imagine:

    Vegetable and Chicken Broths

    Organic Vegetable and Chicken Broths

Shari Ann's: 365 Organic

    Chicken Broth

    Organic Vegetable Broth

    Chicken Noodle Soup with Roasted Garlic

    Pintos with Roasted Green Chili and Lime

Hain's:

    Black Bean

    Chicken Broth

Vegetarian Lentil

Vegetarian Split Pea

Shelton's:

Chicken Broth

Beans and Rice

Turkey Chili

Black Bean Chili

## Jams and Sauces

Fiordilfrutta: Apricot, Peach, Wild Berries, Wild Blueberry,
   Raspberry, Cranberry, Cherry

Bionaturae: Bilberries, Apricot, Peach, Plum, Strawberry

Knudsen's or Kime's Apple Butter

Whole Foods' Organic Unsweetened Applesauce

Santa Cruz Organic Apple Apricot, Apple Blackberry, Apple
   Cherry, Apple Cinnamon Sauces

## Salad Dressings

I have yet to find a commercial salad dressing that doesn't have
vinegar and/or sugar in it. But I'll keep looking. Homemade is much
better, anyway.

## Spaghetti Sauces

Enrico's All Natural

Eden Spaghetti Sauce

Pomi Chunky Tomato w/onion, basil & garlic

Mellina's Finest:

Organic Sweet Pepper and Onion Pasta Sauce

Organic Marinara Pasta Sauce

Organic Tomato and Basil Pasta Sauce

Mom's Spaghetti Sauce

Mama Cocco's Marinara Spaghetti Sauce

Muir Glen's "Outrageously Delicious Organic Pasta Sauce"

Uncle Dave's Excellent Marinara Chunky Tomato Pasta Sauce

Tasty Tomato Basil and Garlic Spaghetti Sauce

Tree of Life's Tomato Sauce

## Milk Substitutes

Almond milk

Coconut Milk

Hemp Milk

Rice Milk

Oat Milk

Better Than Milk

Pacific Ultra Rice Dream

## Cereals, Dry:

Apple Cinnamon O's from Lifestream

Rusketts, from La Loma

Uncle Sam

Puffed Kashi from Kashi-Co.

Spelt Flakes

"Oatios" from New Morning

Puffed Wheat

Puffed Millet

Nature Puffs

Oat Bran Flakes

## Cereals, Hot

Arrowhead Mills:

McCann's Steel Cut Irish Oatmeal

Rice and Shine

Wheatena

Seven Grain

Roman Meal cereal

## Mixes

Bob's Wheat-Free Biscuit and Baking Mix

The Gluten-Free Pantry's Perfect Pie Crust Mix

Up Country Natural's Multi-Grain Pancake and Waffle Mix

## Chips and Salsas

Garden of Eatin':

Green Mountain Gringo Tortilla Chips

Black Bean Tortilla Chips Terra Chips

Mini-Corn Chips

Corntilla Chips

Hain's:

   Sesame Blues

   Sesame Tortilla Chips

   Sunflower Blues

Whole Foods:

   Sweet Potato Chips

   Salsa and Salsa Verde

   Blue Corn Chips

   Lundberg:

      Organic Chili

      Rice Chips (Sea Salt)

      Black Bean and Spicy Chili

## Pickles

Bubbies Pure Kosher Dills

## Crackers

Blue Diamond Pecan Thins

Carr's Table Water Crackers

Sesmark Rice Thins

Wasa Light Rye Crsipbread

Whole Food's Woven Wheats

Courtney's Water Crackers

Edward & Son's Brown Rice Snaps (Onion Garlic)

Hain's Apple Cinnamon and Popcorn Rice Cakes

Lundberg's Wild Rice and Brown Rice Cakes

Blue Diamond Hazelnut Thins
Blue Diamond Almond Thins
Mighty Mo Munchies (cajun)

## Yeast-Free Breads:

Monterey Organic Sourdough Bread
Rudolph's Rye
Essene Breads:
The Fillo Factory: Five Seed        Organic Pastry Shells
Multi-Grain Grain Tortillas:
Alvarado St. Bakery's Sprouted Wheat Tortillas
Food for Life Ezekial 4:9 Sprouted Grain Tortillas

# In The Grocery Store

## Spreads and Sauces

Tap'n Apple apple butter spread
Joyva Sesame Tahini
Laura Scudder Peanut Butter
Camp's 100% Pure Maple Syrup

## Spaghetti Sauces:

Hunt's Tomato Sauce
Classico Spicy Red Pepper and Sweet Pepper and Onion
Aldo Vesuvio Tasty Tomato Basil and Garlic
Hunt's Classico Italian Garlic and Herb, and Tomato Basil
Hunt's All Natural Tomatoes
Rao's Homemade Marinara Sauce

## Dried Soup Mixes:

Bean Cuisine soup mixes and many others

## Canned Soups and Beans:

Casa Fiesta Refried Beans

Progresso Lentil Soup
Pritikin Chicken Broth
Rosarita Vegetarian Refried Beans

## Chips

Lay's Potato Chips
La Costena's Green Mexican Salsa
El Galindo tortilla chips
Embesa's Salsa Mexicana and Salsa Verde
Tostitos tortilla chips
Herdez Salsa Caser
Utz's Kettle Classic Potato Chips

## Fruits and Juices

Walnut Acres Peach and Apple Juices
Treetop Unsweetened Applesauce
White House Natural Plus Applesauce
Mott's Natural Applesauce
Dole Pineapple Chunks
Del Monte Pineapple in its own juices
V-8 Juice
Tree Top Apple Juice
Martinelli Apple Juice
Ocean Spray 100% Grapefruit Juice

## Crackers

Ryvita's Toasted
Kavli Crispbreads
Sesmark's Rice Thins
Manischewitz Matsos
Carr's Table Water Crackers
Lawry's Taco Shells
RyKrisps
Sesame Rye

Triscuits Whole Wheat and Reduced Fat

Quaker Rice Cakes and Butter Pop Corn Cakes

Hol-Grain Brown Rice and Whole Wheat Crackers

## Cereals

Puffed Kashi

Nabisco Shredded Wheat and Spoon Size Shredded Wheat

Wheatena

Hodgson Mill Oat Bran

Aunt Jemima Grits, old fashioned or quick cooking

Old Fashioned Quaker Oats and Multi-Grain

CHAPTER IV

# Tips

*"The kitchen and the oratory are equally holy."*

—ST. BENEDICT

1. Fill a small spray bottle with Bragg's Liquid Aminos, and spray a small amount on popcorn instead of using butter. Add garlic powder if desired. Less calories, different and delicious.

2. Don't buy juices in cartons that are lined with foil. They tend to be contaminated with yeast. Buy juices in glass jars, and dilute half with water the first month.

3. Squeeze fresh lemon juice into your drinking water. Lemon is healing to the liver, and will help speed up detoxification. Alkalizing also.

4. Get out the crock pot! It is so wonderful for cooking chicken, turkey, lamb, stews, oatmeal, beans, grains, etc. Crock pot cooking is one of the most nutritious ways of cooking.

5. Be sure to check all your vitamin and mineral preparations to make sure they don't contain yeast. Buy only natural and yeast-free products.

6. Drink filtered, mineral or spring water only. Never drink distilled water. It leaches valuable minerals from the body. 2 quarts pure water daily.

7.    Wash cantaloupe skin and strawberries carefully before cutting into them. Their skins are porous and may harbor mold.

8.    Eat leftovers in the refrigerator within two days.

9.    Use oatmeal instead of bread crumbs when called for.

10.   Use water chestnuts instead of mushrooms.

11.   Pour apple juice on cereal instead of alternative milks for a change.

12.   *Always* eat breakfast to set your metabolism for the day. This is the best time to eat your one or two pieces of fruit.

13.   *Never* skip a meal. Low blood sugar makes yeast hungry, too.

14.   Do not use yogurt or vinegar douches or coffee enemas under any circumstances.

15.   Substitute canned coconut milk for milk and cream.

16.   Fasting is not allowed. Fasting causes minerals to disappear from blood stream.

17.   If you have allergies to certain foods, rotate your foods so that you don't eat them more frequently than every four or five days.

18.   For patients who are highly allergic to chemicals, make a bath of 1 tsp. Clorox to 1 gallon of water. Soak fruits and vegetables in the bath for 20 min. Rinse thoroughly. (Removes insecticides, preservatives, colorings, metal, salts, fungi and bacteria.)

19.   If you can't find organic chicken, remove skin and sprinkle sea salt over the meat. Let sit 30 min. and rinse carefully. This will remove toxic substances and the taste is delicious. You may want to cut down on salt in your recipe since a small amount will remain in the tissue.

20.   Use only sea salt. It contains more than 80 sea minerals in perfect balance. The trace minerals and macro-nutrients present in naturally harvested sea salt are in a precise dosage identical in composition to that of our body fluids. It is both a food and a medicine. Chemically

produced table salt has been stripped of all of its minerals and nutrients and is unbalanced and harmful. It can legally contain up to 2% chemical additives such as bleaches, anti-caking agents and conditioners. Salt to which iodine has been added contains 20 times the naturally occurring amount in sea salt. Unbalanced and dangerous.

21.  Eat carbohydrates moderately. One portion per meal, please. Yeast learns to eat other carbs after the sugar is taken away. *Do Not* go on a low carbohydrate diet, however. It will shock the system— especially the pancreas and adrenals—and throw it out of balance.

22.  Don't eat irradiated foods. They will stress the immune system further by adding more toxic chemicals to the total body load.

23.  Don't cook with aluminum pots and pans or use aluminum foil. Aluminum dissolves when it touches organic acids and alkalis which are found in fruit and vegetables. Salt and baking soda also speed up corrosion. Once "aluminumized" food is eaten and is dissolved by the hydrochloric acid in the stomach, it enters the bloodstream and is deposited in organs, tissues and muscles. Aluminum has been found in the brains of Alzheimer patients.

24.  Use only aluminum-free baking powder. Rumford is excellent.

25.  Check ingredients in underarm anti-perspirants and deodorants. Most have aluminum and other harmful ingredients. Use Aubrey's E plus High C roll-on deodorant.

26.  Don't panic if a no-no slips into your diet on occasion, either by mistake, or heaven forbid, on purpose. You won't undo everything. Even though you have stimulated a few yeast, if you get right back on the diet and don't feed them, they will die also.

27.  If you can't find a good yeast-free bread, go online and search for yeast-free breads and bakeries. My favorite is Monterey Organic Sourdough. See if your grocer will get it in for you.

28.  If you have arthritis, eliminate members of the nightshade family from your diet. They include white potatoes, peppers, eggplant, tomatoes and tobacco. Be sure to alkalize with a green drink daily. (See tip 31.)

29. Check your urine and saliva pH levels at home with pH strips found in pharmacies. Your body should be slightly alkaline at a pH of 7.365. Yeast loves an acid body and over-acidity causes many of the symptoms of candida.

30. Have a live blood analysis done. You can actually see how your blood is teeming with bacteria, yeast, fungi, mold and other unsavory characters. Very motivating! Your doctor or chiropractor can help you find a live blood test practitioner.

31. Add a "green drink" to your daily regimen to help alkalize your body. Look for one containing a wide variety of grasses, including wheat grass, barley grass, lemon grass, shave grass, kamut grass, oat grass. (If you can't find them, just barley grass will do.) Green drinks help regenerate healthy new cells to replace the ones the yeast-beast ate. Don't buy the ones with algae, probiotics or mushrooms.

32. Try stevia powder to sweeten drinks, fruit sauces, etc. It is an herb that is thirty times sweeter than sugar, does not alter blood sugar levels or feed yeast and has no calories. A little goes a long way. Stevia Plus is excellent.

33. If you smoke, now is the time to *quit* Get that monkey off your back. The largest purchaser of refined sugar in the United States is, of course, the baking industry. The second largest purchaser of refined sugar is the tobacco industry! Flue-cured tobacco contains as much as 20 percent sugar by weight, and even air-cured tobacco has sugar added during the blending process, (plus salt, licorice and salt petre). Every time you inhale you are getting a sugar fix, your blood sugar level rises and the yeast are ecstatic!

34. Use the microwave oven as little as possible. Microwaves destroy enzymes, the vital life force of food. Recent research in Russia proved micowaving increased cancer causing effects, depleted nutritional values and rendered all food acid- forming. Not a good recipe for health. All microwave ovens are now banned in Russia. I don't even own one.

35. Find a good massage therapist and treat yourself to a massage once a week while you are healing. This will help break down the accumulations of toxins and will speed the healing.

36.   Once a week take a soaking bath which will open the pores of the skin and allow toxins to escape. Before bedtime, bring 8 cups of water to a boil, add 2 chamomile tea bags and boil for 15 minutes. Pour tea into a tub full of comfortably hot water, add ⅓ cup sea salt and ⅓ cup hydrogen peroxide. Soak, using no soap, for 20 minutes, rubbing a washcloth in circular motions. Towel off and go to bed. This bath really speeds up healing.

37.   Always remain cheerful while healing yourself. Leave your martyr complex at the back door. Nobody enjoys being around a whiney person.

38.   Find someone who needs help of some kind and offer to help. It will be good for him or her, and good for you, too.

39.   Give yourself a gift and watch faithfully The Doug Kaufmann Show "Know the Cause." on CTN Monday through Friday. It is all about the fungal link to disease. Doug is very knowledgeable and his show will keep you updated on the latest research. Go to www.knowthecause.com to find when the show is on in your area. You can also watch it on the Internet at his website. And while you are there, be SURE to click on and watch "One Man's Hypothesis", Doug's forward thinking presentation on the fungal link to cancer. It is opening eyes and saving lives.

39.   Get plenty of sleep and rest while you heal. Remember the body will be using much energy to detoxify and rebuild itself. You may feel real fatigue the first days or weeks, so keep exercise to a minimum. Use this as a time to nourish, balance, and heal the whole person, body, mind and soul.

40.   Pray daily for the healing to be complete. Learn to meditate and reconnect with our Creator. All healing is simply activating the God within.

*Lord, for what we are about to receive, make us truly thankful.*

*And for the struggles of this life, make us strong and worthy.*

*And for the beauties in this world and the love in this room,*

*Make us humble and grateful."*

—ANON

# Breads, Cereals and Pancakes

*"Let us keep the feast not with the old yeast, the yeast of malice and wickedness, but with bread without yeast, the bread of sincerity and truth. "*

—I CORINTHIANS 5:8

B read may be the staff of life, but our modern-day breads are far from the healthful, nutritious loaves of our ancestors. The bakers' yeast used today is much stronger than that used in past centuries, producing a light, airy bread with holes so big you can see downtown through them! The modern milling process of turning a whole grain flour into a denuded white flour removes twenty-two nutrients from the grain, and the government mandates that three of the B vitamins be replaced, plus vitamin D, calcium, and iron salts, (all synthetic, of course). So, "enriched" flour is a poor substitute for whole grain flour, and I use very little of it.

In recent years a wonderful new grain called Spelt has been rediscovered and cultivated. Its origins go back 8,000 years to Europe, and many people who are allergic to wheat are finding they can tolerate spelt, probably because it is pure and unhybridized, unlike modern grains. It is delicious and has become my whole grain flour of choice. It comes in whole wheat and white.

Most of your favorite recipes for muffins, biscuits, and baking powder breads are easily adapted to yeast-free cooking. Just substitute alternative milks for milk, and if the recipe calls for sugar, either skip it, or substitute a little honey, maple syrup, or stevia.

In a lot of my recipes you will see that sometimes I use half alternative milk and half water. That is because some of the alternative milks are thicker than others. In some recipes a thicker milk works better. See which you prefer. I usually use coconut milk and Rice Dream full strength. In recipes calling for cream I use canned coconut milk. The thickest part of canned coconut milk even whips when cold from the refrigerator.

Alternative flours like coconut flour, millet flour, tapioca flour, and almond flour are now easy to find. They are delicious and much more nourishing than regular grain flours. Start by using half alternative flour and half regular grain flour and find a balance you like. I am not afraid of the occasional use of white, unbleached flour either.

Here are a few of my family's favorite bread recipes.

*Basic Yeast Free Bread (p. 41)*

## Basic Yeast-Free Bread

3 cups **flour**–organic if possible–all kinds
4 tsp. **baking powder**
2 tsp. **sea salt**
1 ½ cups **rice milk, almond milk, coconut milk,** *or* **water**
¼ cup melted **butter** or light **olive oil**

1. Mix flour, baking powder and salt.
2. Mix liquids and add to dry. Stir well. Dough should be moist but not sticky.
3. Shape into ball or oval with oiled hands. Do not overwork.
4. Place on parchment paper on a baking sheet.
5. Score lightly with an X shape to prevent crust from splitting.
6. Bake for 40 minutes at 400*

*Variations on this recipe are endless. I have made it with half oatmeal, used tomato juice and marinated dried tomatoes, apple juice and apples, half whole wheat flour and half white, added herbs, oiled the top with olive oil and sprinkled the top with sea salt and oregano to make a focaccia, etc. Use your imagination.*

*This is a country style bread that should be sliced thick. Great toasted.*

## Grits Muffins

1 cup cold cooked baked **grits**, (p. 121)
½ cup **almond, rice, hemp,** *or* **coconut milk**
(cartoned, not canned)
½ cup **water**
1 cup unbleached white **flour**
4 tsp. Rumford **baking powder**
½ tsp. **sea salt**
2 **eggs**, well-beaten

*Makes 12*

*Freezes well.*

*Leftover cooked millet and quinoa make equally delicious muffins.*

1. Add water and milk to grits to soften. Mash well with fork.
2. Mix flour, baking powder and salt, and add to grits.
3. Add eggs lightly—do not beat.
4. Pour into greased muffin tins and bake at 425° for 25 min.

# Cornbread

*This recipe is easily doubled, using a 10" skillet. It freezes well, and is wonderful leftover for breakfast.*

1 cup organic stone ground **yellow corn meal**
½ cup **almond milk**
½ cup **water**
1 **egg**
2 tsp. Rumford **baking powder**
¾ tsp. **sea salt**
2 T. extra-light **olive oil**

1. Turn on oven to 475°. Place an 8" iron skillet (mandatory) in oven to get piping hot.

2. In a small bowl, whisk together the egg, almond milk, and water.

3. In a large bowl, mix together the corn meal, baking powder, and salt.

4. Mix the egg mixture into the cornmeal mixture, stirring just until blended

5. Carefully remove hot skillet from oven, add oil, swirling oil around to coat bottom and sides of skillet. Pour hot oil into cornmeal mixture, stir lightly, and pour mixture into hot skillet.

6. Bake 20 minutes. Cut into 6 pieces immediately, and serve with butter.

# Vera's Bread

*Rich, tasty and nutritious. Will help replace lots of the vitamins and minerals the yeast-beasts ate.*

1 ½ cups **unbleached white flour**
1 ½ cups **whole wheat** *or* **spelt flour**
2 tsp. Rumford **baking powder**
1 tsp. **baking soda**
½ tsp. **sea salt**
½ cup **sesame seeds**
½ cup **bulgur wheat**
¼ cup **flax seeds**
¼ cup **sunflower seeds**, roasted
1 T. **oat bran** *or* **wheat germ**

2 cups plus 2 T. **almond milk**

3 T. **honey**

---

1. Sift flours, baking powder, soda, and salt into large bowl.

2. Stir in sesame seeds, sunflower seeds, flax seeds, bulgur wheat and oat bran.

3. In a small bowl, mix honey into the almond milk.

4. Add almond milk mixture to flour mixture, stirring lightly just until blended.

5. Pour into greased 9" x 5" bread pan and bake at 325° for 1 hr. 15 min. to 30 min. Check to make sure it's done.

6. Turn out onto rack to cool, and butter or oil top of bread.

## Spoon Bread

---

1 ½ cups **almond milk**

1 ½ cups **water**

1 cup organic stone-ground **yellow corn meal**

1 ½ tsp. **sea salt**

2 T. **butter**

4 **egg yolks**, beaten

4 **egg whites**, beaten

---

*Serves 4-6*

*This is really a fallen souffle, and was traditionally served in bowls and eaten with a spoon. A southern favorite.*

1. In a 2 qt. saucepan, combine milk, water, corn meal, and salt. Cook over medium heat, stirring constantly, until thickened.

2. Mix in butter and let cool to lukewarm.

3. Beat egg yolks and stir into cornmeal mixture.

4. Beat egg whites until stiff but not dry, and fold carefully into cornmeal mixture.

5. Pour into greased 2 qt. casserole, and bake at 400° 35 - 40 min. until browned and set.

6. Serve immediately with butter, in small bowls if you like.

# Biscuits

2 cups flour: **unbleached white, spelt, whole wheat** *or* **half and half**
2 heaping tsp. Rumford **baking powder**
1 tsp. **sea salt**
4 heaping T. organic **coconut oil**
¾ cup **almond** *or* **rice milk**

1   Sift flour, baking powder and sea salt in large bowl.

2.  Cut in coconut oil with pastry blender or knife until mixture resembles coarse meal.

3.  Add milk and mix quickly with a fork until blended. Add a little more milk if mixture seems dry.

4.  Drop by large spoonsful onto baking sheet and bake 15 - 18 min. at 450°.

# Herbed Scones

*Makes 12*

2 ½ cups **unbleached flour**
2 tsp. Rumford **baking powder**
1 tsp. **dried rosemary**
½ tsp. each: **baking soda, sea salt, dried thyme, and dried sage**
½ cup cold **butter**
1 **egg**
½ cup **almond milk**
½ cup **water**

1.  In a large bowl combine flour, baking powder, rosemary, soda, salt, thyme, and sage.

2.  Cut in butter with knife until butter is in very small pieces.

3.  Beat egg with water and milk, and stir into flour. Mix until blended.

4.  Either roll out on floured board and cut with large biscuit cutter, or

drop using large spoon onto lightly greased baking sheet 1" apart.

5. Brush with melted butter if desired, and

6. bake at 400° 20 - 25 min.

## Rice Muffins

---

1 cup **cooked rice—white** or **brown**
½ cup **almond milk**
½ cup **water**
5 T. melted **butter** ½ tsp. **sea salt**
2 **eggs**, well beaten
3 tsp. Rumford **baking powder**
1 ½ cups **flour, unbleached white,**
**whole wheat,** or **spelt,** or **half each**

---

*Makes 12*

1. Sift dry ingredients and mix into rice.

2. Beat eggs, almond milk and add water. Pour into rice and

   flour mixture.

3. Add melted butter, and mix into a soft batter, stirring lightly but

   thoroughly.

4. Pour into greased muffin tins, and bake at 450° 18 - 20 min.

## Morning Bread

---

1 cup **oatmeal**
1 cup **whole wheat flour, brown rice flour,** or **spelt flour**
1 cup **unbleached white flour**
2 tsp. Rumford **baking powder**
½ tsp. **baking soda**
1 tsp. **sea salt**
½ cup **almond** or **rice milk**
½ cup **water**
¼ cup extra-light **olive oil**

*This is one of the most versatile of my baking powder bread recipes.*

*You can use 3 cups of any flours. Have fun experimenting. Sometimes I use bran, or wheat germ, or rye flour for a different taste. You can also find white spelt flour. This bread is rich and crumbly, and is so good warm for breakfast, with apple butter and herb tea.*

¼ cup **honey** *or* **pure maple syrup**
1 **egg**

---

1. In a large bowl mix together the oatmeal, flours, baking powder soda, and salt.
2. In a small bowl mix together the almond milk, water, oil, honey, and egg.
3. Stir liquid mixture into the flour mixture lightly.
4. Pour into greased 9" x 5" pan, and bake at 350° 50 minutes.

## Craig's Bread

---

3 cups **flour**
2 tsp. **baking powder**
1 tsp. **baking soda**
1 tsp. **sea salt** *or* **seasoned salt**
1 cup **veggie pulp**
1 ½ cups **coconut** *or* **almond milk**
1 **egg**, beaten
¼ cup extra-virgin **olive oil**

---

*We have a wonderful juicer that extracts pulp. It always bothered me to throw that nutritious, fiber-laden pulp away, so son Craig came up with this delicious recipe to help. Extra pulp can be frozen and used later. So good warm from the oven with butter...mmm.*

1. Sift together the flour, baking powder, baking soda, and salt.
2. Mix in the veggie pulp
3. Mix together the milk, egg, and olive oil.
4. Bake at 350* for one hour.

## Blueberry Muffins

---

¾ cup **whole wheat** *or* **spelt flour**
¾ cup **unbleached white flour**
½ cup stone ground **yellow cornmeal**

1 T. Rumford **baking powder**
½ tsp. **sea salt**
6 T. extra-light **olive oil**
1 **egg**, beaten
1 cup **almond milk** *or* Rice Dream
⅓ cup pure **maple syrup**
1 cup fresh or frozen **blueberries**

_____

*Makes 12*

*The best you'll ever eat!*

*Strawberries, black-berries and raspberries are equally yummy.*

1.  Sift or mix flours, cornmeal, baking powder and salt.

2.  In small bowl, mix oil, egg, almond milk and maple syrup. Stir mixtures together lightly.

3.  Add blueberries and spoon into oiled muffin tins.

4.  Bake at 375° for 25 min. or until golden brown.

## Almond Bread

_____

2 cups **whole wheat flour,** *or* 1 cup **whole wheat,** 1 cup **unbleached white**
½ cup **bran flakes**
1 tsp. **sea salt**
½ tsp. Rumford **baking soda**
½ tsp. **baking powder**
2 **eggs**, slightly beaten
½ cup **water**
½ cup **almond milk**
2 tsp. pure **almond extract**
¼ cup finely chopped **almonds**
¼ cup **honey**

_____

1.  In a large bowl, combine flour, bran flakes, salt, soda and baking powder.

2.  In a small bowl, combine eggs, water, almond milk, almond extract, and honey.

3. Add liquid ingredients to the flour mixture.

4. Stir in nuts.

5. Pour batter into greased 9" x 5" loaf pan.

6. Bake 375° for 40 - 50 min., or until done.

## Wheat-Free Bread or Muffins

---

*People with or without wheat allergies will enjoy these.*

*Can also be baked in an 8 ½" x 4 ½" pan 50-55 min., or in muffin tins for 12.*

1 ½ cup **oat bran**
¾ cup stone-ground **yellow cornmeal**
1 tsp. **sea salt**
2 tsp. Rumford **baking powder**
2 cups **almond milk**
2 T. pure **maple syrup**
1 large **egg**, beaten
1 T. extra-light **olive** *or* melted **coconut oil**
¼ cup **sunflower seeds** (optional)

---

1. In a medium bowl, mix together the oat bran, cornmeal, salt and baking powder.

2. In another bowl, beat egg, almond milk, maple syrup and oil.

3. Mix the two mixtures together very lightly. Mixture will be soupy.

4. Pour into a greased 8" square baking pan and bake at 425°
   20 - 25 min. or until done.

## Sesame Drop Biscuits

---

*Makes 12*

1 cup **unbleached white flour** and 1 cup **whole wheat flour**
1 ½ tsp. Rumford **baking powder**
½ tsp. **baking soda**
½ tsp. **sea salt**
½ cup **butter**

4 T. **sesame seeds**
½ cup **almond milk**
½ cup **water**

---

1. In large bowl stir together flour, baking powder, soda, and salt.

2. Cut in butter with knife or pastry blender until butter is in small pieces. Stir in seeds.

3. Mix milk and water and add to flour mixture. Stir lightly with a fork.

4. Drop by tablespoons onto greased cookie sheet.

5. Bake at 450° 12 - 14 min.

## Zucchini Bread

---

3 **eggs**
1 cup pure **maple syrup**
½ cup extra-light **olive oil**
1 tsp. pure **vanilla extract**
grated rind of 1 **lemon**
1 ¾ cup grated **zucchini**
1 ½ cup **unbleached white flour**
1 cup whole **wheat** *or* **spelt flour**
1 T. Rumford **baking powder**
½ tsp. **sea salt**

---

*This is fabulous—more of a cake than a bread. Try it warm with a little butter.*

1. Beat eggs well, and slowly add maple syrup, oil, vanilla and lemon rind. Stir in zucchini which has been lightly squeezed in paper towels.

2. In a large bowl, mix together the flours, baking powder and salt.

3. Stir in egg/zucchini mixture, blending just until smooth.

4. Bake at 350° in a 9" x 5" greased pan for 50 - 60 minutes or until done.

5. Cool in pan for 5 - 10 minutes and turn out onto rack to cool.

## Oat Crackers

*When you can't find yeast-free crackers, make your own!*

*If your cookie sheets have no sides, you can roll the dough out right on top of them.*

3 cups **rolled oats**
2 cups **unbleached white flour**
1 cup **oat bran** *or* **wheat germ**
1 tsp. **sea salt**
1 T. pure **maple syrup**
⅔ cup extra-light **olive oil**
1 cup **water**

1   In large bowl, mix together oats, flour, oat bran and salt.

2.   In small bowl, mix maple syrup, oil and water. Add to oat mixture.

3.   Form into three uniform balls and roll each into 9″ x 13″ rectangles to fit into cookie sheets of that size. Place in greased cookie sheets.

4.   Sprinkle lightly with salt and score the dough into squares.

5.   Bake 20 min. at 350°. Check outer crackers early and remove them if they are too brown. Crackers should be light brown.

## Dessert Shortcakes

*Serves 6*

2 cups **unbleached white flour**
3 tsp. Rumford **baking powder**
⅓ cup chilled **butter**
½ tsp. **sea salt**
½ tsp. pure **vanilla extract** *or* **nutmeg**
⅔ cup **almond milk**—more if needed

1.   Mix together flour, baking powder, salt.

2.   Cut in butter with a pastry blender or knife until evenly blended.

3.   Add vanilla to almond milk and gradually add to butter-flour mixture, mixing just long enough to form a soft dough.

4.   Roll out dough on a floured surface to ½″ thickness. Cut into 12 3″ rounds and place on buttered baking sheet.

5.  Bake at 425° for 12 min. or until just lightly browned.

6.  Slice in half, butter lightly, and pour cherry pie mixture (p.168) over halves. .

## Spicy Oatmeal

4 T. **apple juice**
1 ½ cups **water**
⅔ cup **rolled oats**
2 **apples**, peeled, cored and finely chopped
½ cup chopped **pecans**
1 T. **wheat germ**
½ tsp. **ginger**
¼ tsp. **cloves**
1 tsp. **cinnamon**
½ tsp. **sea salt**

*Serves 4*

1.  Combine all ingredients in a saucepan and bring to a boil.

2.  Reduce heat and simmer 8 - 10 min. Remove heat, cover and let stand several minutes before serving.

3.  Top with maple syrup and almond milk.

## Granola

3 cups **oats**
1 cup **wheat germ**
1 cup **unsweetened coconut** (from health food store)
1 cup **pecans**, chopped
½ cup **raw sesame seeds**
½ cup **raw sunflower seeds**
¾ cup **honey**
¼ cup extra-light **olive**
1 tsp. pure **vanilla extract**

*For a change, substitute almonds and almond extract.*

1. Mix oats, wheat germ, coconut, pecans, sesame seeds, and sunflower seeds in a large bowl.

2. In a small bowl, mix together the oil, honey and vanilla. Stir into oat mixture.

3. Bake at 350° for 30 min., stirring every 5 - 10 min.

4. Cool completely and store in air-tight container.

## Oatmeal Scones

---

1 cup **quick-cooking oats**
1 cup **unbleached white flour**
4 tsp. Rumford **baking powder**
½ tsp. **sea salt**
½ cup **butter** *or* organic **coconut oil**
⅔ cup **rice** *or* **almond milk**

---

*Makes 12*

*These are crumbly, but oh-so-good. Remember, no more than two, and no other carbohydrates with the meal.*

1. Cook the oats in an ungreased skillet over moderate heat for 5 - 6 min. or until lightly browned. Set aside.

2. Sift the flour, baking powder and salt into a bowl. Cut in butter with a pastry blender or knife until mixture resembles coarse meal. Stir in oatmeal.

3. Add milk and stir to make a soft dough.

4. Drop by spoonfuls onto a lightly greased cookie sheet and bake 12 - 15 min. at 425°

## Oatmeal Pancakes with Honey-Butter Syrup

---

1 ½ cups **oats**
1 cup **almond** *or* **rice milk**

1 cup **water**
1 cup **flour, unbleached white,** *or* **whole wheat**
1 T. **honey**
2 ½ tsp. Rumford **baking powder**
1 tsp. **sea salt**
2 **eggs**, well-beaten
¼ cup extra-light **olive** *or* **liquid coconut oil**

*Serves 4*

*A family favorite. For those on the diet, make every two weeks at most.*

1. Pour water and milk over oats and let sit for 5 min.

2. Sift flour, baking powder and salt. Stir in lightly.

3. Add eggs, oil and honey, and bake on greased griddle.

4. Serve with maple syrup, or make a delicious honey syrup by melting 4 T. butter, add 1 cup honey and 1 tsp. vanilla. Serve warm.

## Spicy Pancakes

1 cup **whole wheat flour**
2 tsp. Rumford **baking powder**
2 T. **honey**
½ tsp. ground **allspice**
¼ tsp. ground **nutmeg**
1 **egg**, lightly beaten
½ cup **water**
½ cup **almond** *or* **rice milk**
2 T. extra-light **olive oil**
½ tsp. **sea salt**

*Serves 3*

1. Combine flour, baking powder, honey, salt, allspice and nutmeg in a large bowl.

2. In a small bowl, beat egg, add water, milk and oil.

3. Add to flour mixture and let stand 5 - 10 min.

4. Bake on greased griddle until done.

## Happy Apple Pancakes

---

1 large or 2 small **apples**, peeled, cored and chopped fine
2 cups **flour**
1 T. **honey**
2 tsp. **vanilla**
2 tsp. **baking powder**
½ tsp. **sea salt**
2 **eggs**, well beaten
⅓ cup **coconut** *or* light **olive oil**
2 cups **almond milk**

---

1. Sift together the flour, baking powder, and salt.

2. Blend eggs, oil, almond milk, and vanilla.

3. Add dry ingredients and fold in chopped apples.

4. Cook on heated and oiled griddle and serve with pure maple syrup.

## Blueberry Brancakes

---

*Serves 4*

2 cups **whole wheat flour** *or* **spelt flour**
1 cup **unprocessed bran**
1 T. Rumford **baking powder**
1 tsp. **sea salt**
1 tsp. ground **cinnamon**
2 cups **almond** *or* **rice milk**
2 **eggs**
½ cup **honey**
¼ cup extra-light **olive oil**
½ - 1 cup fresh or unthawed, frozen **blueberries**

---

1. In large bowl, mix together the flour, bran, baking powder, salt
   and cinnamon.

2. In small bowl, combine the milk, eggs, honey and oil. Stir lightly
   into flour mixture.

3. Let stand 2 - 3 min., then fold in blueberries.

4. Pour about ¼ cup batter for each pancake onto preheated griddle and brown on both sides. Serve immediately with honey-butter syrup (p. 53) .

## Perfect Pumpkin Pancakes

1 cup **multi-grain pancake and waffle mix** (I like Arrowhead Mills)
1 T. **maple syrup**
1 T. melted organic **coconut oil**
¾ cup **canned pumpkin**
1 tsp. **sea salt**
1 tsp. **cinnamon**
¼ tsp. **nutmeg**
1 large **egg**
1 cup **water**

*Serves 3-4*

1. Combine pancake mix salt and spices in medium size bowl.
2. In separate bowl whisk together egg and maple syrup, then add pumpkin, oil and water.
3. Mix wet and dry ingredients to make batter.
4. Bake on greased griddle, turning once.

## Basic Waffles

1 ½ cups any **flour**
¼ tsp. **sea salt**
1 T. Rumford **baking powder**
1 ¾ cup **almond** *or* **rice milk**
¼ cup extra-light **olive oil**
1 T. **honey** *or* **pure maple syrup**

*Serves 4*

1. In a large bowl, combine flour, salt and baking powder.
2. In small bowl, combine egg, milk, oil and honey. Add to flour

mixture, mixing lightly.

3.  Bake in hot waffle iron. Top with raspberry syrup.

## Raspberry Syrup

*Strawberries and blue-berries are delicious also.*

*Good hot or cold.*

1 (12 oz.) package frozen **unsweetened raspberries**
¼ cup **unsweetened apple juice**
2 tsp. **cornstarch**
1 tsp. freshly squeezed **lemon juice**
½ cup **honey**

1.  Combine all ingredients in saucepan.
2.  Cook over medium heat until syrup thickens.

# Soups

*"Put on the cooking pot, put it on and pour water into it. Cook the meat well, mixing in the spices."*

—EZEKIEL 24:3-4

## Chicken and Rice Soup

*Serves 8*

*A long-time family favorite.*
*Sesame Drop Biscuits are*
*good with this.*

1 whole **chicken**
8 cups **water**
1 tsp. **sea salt**
2 stalks **celery** with tops
½ medium **onion**, chopped
1 cup **carrots,** chopped
1 cup **celery,** *or* **broccoli** chopped
1 cup **zucchini** *or* **yellow squash,** sliced
1 cup **basmati rice**
1 T. **Herbamare**
1 tsp. **black pepper**
1 T. **cumin**
1 T. **dried oregano**
1 bunch **cilantro,** chopped

1.  Cook chicken in water with salt, celery and tops, and onion for one hour or until done. Remove from broth, cool, and debone.
2.  Cook rice in 2 cups of the chicken broth 20 min. or until done.
3.  While rice is cooking, add carrots, celery, zucchini, Herbamare, pepper, cumin and oregano to the remaining chicken broth and cook covered for 10 min.
4.  Combine all in a large pan, add cilantro and cook a few more minutes.

## White Bean Soup with Kale and Turkey Sausage

*Serves 4-6*

1 T. **extra-virgin olive oil**
8 oz. raw **sweet Italian turkey sausage**
2 cups chopped **sweet onion**
6 **garlic** cloves, minced
6 cups **chicken broth**
4 cans **cannellini beans,** rinsed and drained
8 cups chopped **kale**

1 tsp. freshly ground **black pepper**

**Herbamare** to taste

---

1. Heat the oil in a large pan and cook the sausage, onions, and garlic for 5 - 7 minutes or until tender.
2. Add broth, beans and pepper. Cook 3 - 5minutes. Use a masher to partially mash it up.
3. Stir in kale and cook 6 - 8 more minutes. Add black pepper.

## Lentil Spinach Soup

---

2 cups **lentils**

10 cups **water**

2 cups **onions**, chopped

1 cup **celery** and tops, chopped

1 cup chopped **carrots**

2 cloves **garlic**, crushed

1 tsp. **dried thyme**

1 lb. fresh **spinach**

1 (1 lb.) can **Italian plum tomatoes**

2 T. **Herbamare**

1 tsp. **black pepper**

¼ cup extra-virgin **olive oil**

---

*Serves 6-8*

*I love lentils, as you can see. They are quick to cook, very nutritious, and low carb also. Here are three soups you may enjoy.*

1. Place lentils, water, onion, celery, carrots, garlic and thyme in large pot, bring to a boil, cover and cook on low for 1 hour.
2. Chop fresh spinach into bite-sized pieces and add with tomatoes to lentil mixture, simmer 20 min.
3. Season with Herbamare, pepper and olive oil. .

## Curried Lentil Soup

---

1 T. extra-virgin **olive oil**

1 large **onion,** chopped

*Cornbread and a tossed*
*green salad are so good*
*with this soup.*

5 cups **water** *or* **chicken broth**
1 cup **lentils**
4 **scallions,** chopped
1 **celery** stalk with top, chopped
1 **carrot,** chopped
1 tsp. ground **coriander**
1 tsp. **turmeric**
1 tsp. **cumin**
1 tsp. **paprika**
⅛ tsp. **cayenne**
¼ tsp. **ginger**
1 T. **Bragg's Liquid Aminos**
½ tsp. **Herbamare**
½ cup **cilantro,** chopped

---

1.  Saute onion in oil until transparent.

2.  Add water, lentils, scallions, celery, carrot, coriander, turmeric, cumin, paprika, cayenne, ginger, Bragg's and Herbamare.

3.  Bring to a boil, lower heat and cook on low 1 hour, or until lentils are soft.

4.  Add cilantro a few minutes before serving.

## Lentil Soup with Lemon Zest

---

*When you need a fabulous*
*soup in a hurry.*
*Delicious hot and cold!*

2 T. extra-virgin **olive oil,** plus more for drizzling
1 large **yellow onion,** thinly sliced
3 **plum tomatoes,** cored and chopped
3 cloves **garlic,** minced
1 tsp. **cumin**
½ tsp. **smoked paprika**
1 (15 oz.) can **lentils,** drained
2 ¼ cups **chicken broth**
Zest and juice of 1 **lemon**
1 tsp. **Herbamare** and **black pepper** to taste

---

1.  In a large saucepan, heat oil over medium heat. Add the onion, garlic, tomatoes and sauté until the onions are soft—about 6 min.

2. Add the cumin and paprika and cook for another minute, stirring constantly.

3. Add lentils and chicken broth and bring to a simmer. Cook for 10 min.

4. Puree in batches in blender or food processor. Return soup to saucepan.

5. Stir in lemon zest and juice, and season with salt and pepper. Return to a simmer.

6. Ladle into soup bowls, and drizzle a little olive oil on top.

## Zucchini Soup

1 ½ lb. **zucchini**
½ medium **onion,** chopped
1 can yeast-free **chicken broth**
½ stick **butter**
1 tsp. **Herbamare**

*Serves 4*

*This is a staple in our house. It's wonderful hot or cold.*

*This can be made with broccoli, carrots, cauliflower, almost any vegetable. Add curry for a change of pace. Add 1 tsp. nutmeg to broccoli and cauliflower soups.*

1. Cook zucchini and onion in 1 cup water until done.
2. Put in blender or food processor, add chicken broth and puree.
3. Add butter and Herbamare and blend again.

## Gazpacho

1 large **tomato,** peeled and seeded if necessary
½ **onion,** quartered
½ **cucumber**
½ **green pepper**
1 large **celery** stalk and top
2 tsp. **parsley**
1 tsp. **chives,** fresh or frozen
1 or two cloves **garlic,** minced
2 cups **organic vegetable juice**
3 T. **lemon juice**
2 T. extra-virgin **olive oil**
1 tsp. **Herbamare**

*Serves 4 - 6*

¼ tsp. **black pepper**

1 T. **Bragg's Liquid Aminos**

---

1. Mix in blender or food processor.

2. Chill until very cold, at least three hours.

## Cream of Potato Soup

*Serves 5-6*

2 T. extra-light **olive oil**

1 large **onion,** diced

2 cups **chicken broth**

3 medium **russet potatoes,** peeled and thinly sliced

½ tsp. **dried dill weed**

½ cup **cilantro,** chopped

1 tsp. **Herbamare**

½ tsp. **black pepper**

1 cup **almond** *or* **canned coconut milk**

---

1. In a saucepan, saute onions until they are translucent.

2. Add water, potatoes, dill, Herbamare and pepper and cook until potatoes are soft.

3. Whip soup in blender or food processor until smooth and return to saucepan on low heat. Add cilantro and milk and heat through.

4. Adjust seasonings.

## Split Pea Soup

*Serves 4-6*

2 cups **dried split peas**

2 qts. **water** (I use two cans of **chicken broth** as part of liquid)

1 T. **extra-virgin olive oil**

1 med. **onion**

1 tsp. **garlic** powder

1 T. **Herbamare**
1 T. **cumin**
2 T. **Bragg's Liquid Aminos**
3 stalks chopped **celery**

---

1. Saute onioil until golden.

2. Rinse peas and add all the rest, except celery.

3. Cook covered on low 1 hour.

4. Add celery the last half hour.

## Quick Tortilla Soup

1 lb. (2 large) boneless **chicken breasts,** halved lengthwise to form
two thin cutlets
1 ½ T. **olive oil,** separated
½ tsp. **sea salt**
1 T. **chili powder**
1 large **onion,** chopped
4 cloves **garlic,** crushed
2 T. canned **chipotle peppers in adobe sauce**, minced
2 quarts **chicken broth**
1 (14 ½ oz.) **diced tomatoes** (fire roasted if you can find it)
2 (15 or 16 oz.) **black beans,** not drained
6 oz. **tortilla chips**
1 **lime,** cut into eighths
Sliced **avocado** and chopped **cilantro**—opt.
**Herbamare** to taste

---

1. Heat a Dutch oven or soup kettle over medium-high heat.

2. Toss the chicken with salt, chili powder and 1 ½ tsp. oil to coat.

3. Add chicken to hot pot, cook, turning only once until brown on
   both sides—5 - 6 min. Transfer to a plate and cut into bite-
   sized pieces.

4. Heat remaining oil in the hot empty pot. Add onions and sauté until softened, 4 - 5 min.

5. Add garlic and peppers and cook one minute longer.

6. Add chicken broth, tomatoes, and black beans. Bring to boil, reduce heat to medium-low. Simmer partially covered about five minutes,and skim foam as it surfaces.

7. Stir in chicken and turn off heat.

8. Place a portion of tortilla strips in bowl and ladle over the hot soup. Add fresh lime juice, and top with sliced avocado and chopped cilantro if you like.

## Tarragon Pea Soup

*Serves 6*
*Good hot or cold.*

½ stick **butter**
1 **onion,** chopped
2 large **garlic** cloves, chopped
4 cups **chicken stock** or canned broth
1 large Idaho **potato,** peeled and cut into eighths
1 lb. frozen **petite peas**
¼ tsp. **cayenne pepper**
½ tsp. freshly ground **black pepper**
2 T. **dried tarragon**
1 T. **Herbamare**

1. Melt butter in large saucepan, add onion and garlic and cook gently for 10 min.

2. Add stock and potato and bring to a boil. Reduce heat and cook until potato is just tender, about 15 min.

3. Add the peas, cayenne and pepper and return to a boil. Remove pan from heat and stir in tarragon and Herbamare. Allow soup to cool for 10 min.

4. Process the soup in batches in blender or food processor.

# Greek Lemon-Rice Soup with Chicken

1 quart **chicken broth**
2 boneless skinless **chicken breast halves**, diced
⅓ cup uncooked **long-grained rice**
3 **eggs**
¼ cup fresh **lemon juice**
Sea salt and **pepper** to taste

*Serves 4*

*A simple and very elegant soup—one of my husband's favorites.*

1. Heat the broth over medium-high heat in a large soup pot.

2. Add chicken and rice, cover and cook on low for 15 min. Be careful not to let pot boil over.

3. While the chicken mixture cooks, beat the eggs lightly in a medium bowl. Add the lemon juice and whisk well.

4. When the chicken is tender and the rice is cooked through, remove soup from the heat. Remove 1 cup of broth from the pot and slowly drizzle into egg mixture, whisking constantly.

5. Place the soup back over low heat, and stirring constantly, add the egg mixture to the soup pot. Cook and stir about two minutes to thicken slightly. Do NOT allow soup to boil.

6. Season to taste with salt and pepper. Remove from heat and serve.

# Peanut Butter Soup

1 large stalk **celery** and top, coarsely chopped
1 large **carrot,** coarsely chopped
2 T. chopped **onion**
¾ cup **water**
2 cups **chicken broth,** divided
½ cup natural **creamy peanut butter**
½ tsp. **Herbamare**
¼ tsp. **black pepper**

*Serves 6*

*For peanut butter lovers only.*

*Thin with more chicken broth if too thick and rich for you.*

1 T. **cornstarch**
½ cup **almond** *or* **coconut milk**

---

1. Combine celery, carrots, onion, and 3/4 cup water in a saucepan. Cook covered on low heat for 10 min. or until tender.

2. Add 1 ½ cups chicken broth and pour into food processor.

3. Add peanut butter, Herbamare, and pepper and process until smooth. Return mixture to saucepan.

4. Combine cornstarch and remaining ½ cup chicken broth, stirring until blended. Stir into soup mixture. Bring to a boil, reduce heat to low and cook 1 min.

5. Stir in milk and cook uncovered on low until heated through.

## Cream of Broccoli and Squash Soup

---

4 T. **butter**
1 medium **onion,** chopped
1 large **bay leaf**
2 **garlic** cloves, chopped
3 cups chopped **broccoli**
2 cups **yellow squash,** sliced
1 tsp. **sea salt**
2 cups **water** *or* **vegetable stock**
1 cup **almond** *or* **rice milk**
½ tsp. each: **basil, thyme,** and **marjoram**
¼ tsp. **black pepper**
**Herbamare** to taste

---

*Serves 6-8*

*Sometimes I make this with brussels sprouts instead of broccoli and zucchini instead of yellow squash. Equally good.*

1. In a 3-qt. saucepan, saute onion and garlic in the butter until onions are translucent.

2. Add broccoli, squash, bay leaf, salt and water or stock. Cover and cook 15 min. Remove bay leaf. Puree in blender or food processor.

3. Return to pan, whisk in almond milk, herbs and seasonings, and simmer over low heat for 10 min. Add Herbamare if needed.

## Black Bean Soup Cuban Style

2 cups (1 lb.) **dry black beans**
1 tsp. **sea salt**
8 T. extra-virgin **olive oil**
2 large **onions**, chopped
2 large **green peppers,** chopped
4 large **garlic** cloves, chopped
2 tsp. **cumin**
2 tsp. **oregano**
1 tsp. **Herbamare**
chopped fresh **onion** and **tomato**
**cooked rice**
chopped **cilantro**

*Serves 8*

*Add chopped fresh cilantro just before serving if desired.*

1. Soak beans in 2 qts. water overnight.

2. Add salt, cover and cook until tender—approximately 2 hrs.

3. Saute onions, green pepper, garlic, cumin and oregano in oil until tender. Add to beans and simmer 25 min.

4. Stir in Herbamare and add more if needed. Serve with rice, chopped fresh onions and tomatoes.

## African Vegetable Stew

1 cup **onion**, chopped
½ cup **parsley**, chopped
2 cloves **garlic,** chopped
2 tsp. **cinnamon**
½ tsp. **turmeric**
½ tsp. **black pepper**
½ tsp. **ginger**
2 T. **butter**
5 cups **water**
3 large **carrots**, sliced
½ cup **dried lentils**
1 cup **white rice**
1 (16 oz.) can **tomatoes,** with liquid

*Serves 6-8*

*A thick "potage" full of flavor. Thin with chicken broth if too thick for you.*

1 T. **Herbamare**
1 (10 oz.) pkg. **baby green peas,** frozen
1 (10 oz.) pkg. **green beans,** frozen or fresh if available

---

1. Saute in butter the onion, parsley, garlic, cinnamon, turmeric, pepper and ginger until onion is tender.

2. Add water, carrots and lentils. Heat until the boiling point. Reduce heat and cover. Cook 25 min.

3. Add rice, tomatoes and Herbamare and bring back to the boiling point. Cover and cook on low heat 20 min.

4. Add peas and beans and cook 5 min.


## Mulligatawney Soup

---

*Serves 4*

*I love this recipe—quick and nourishing, and the flavors are wonderful.*

¼ cup **butter**
¼ cup ea. **onion, carrots, celery diced**
1 **green pepper,** chopped fine
1 **apple,** cored and sliced
1 lb. diced or ground **raw chicken** *or* **turkey**
⅓ cup **flour**
2 tsp. **curry powder**
1 tsp. **nutmeg**
4 whole cloves
1 cup chopped, fresh or canned **tomatoes**
5 cups **chicken broth,** canned or homemade
**Sea salt** *or* **Herbamare** and **black pepper** to taste

---

1. In Dutch oven combine butter, onion, carrots, celery, green pepper, apple and chicken. Stir in flour.

2. In a small bowl combine curry, nutmeg, cloves, salt and pepper. Stir into Dutch oven, then add tomatoes and broth.

3. Bring to a boil, cover, reduce heat and simmer 1 hour.

4. Remove from heat and let cool slightly. Puree in a blender if you wish and serve over rice.

## Cauliflower Soup

1 medium head of **cauliflower**
½ cup **onion**
4 cups **chicken broth**
4 T. **butter**
½ tsp. **allspice**
½ tsp. **cardamom**
½ tsp. **cloves**
1 tsp. **celery salt**
½ tsp. **peppercorns**

*Serves 4*

1. Cook cauliflower in butter with onion until nearly done.

2. Add broth and spices and cook a little longer

3. Puree in blender or food processor.

## Cream of Cauliflower and Brussels Sprouts Soup

1 small head **cauliflower,** broken into flowerets
1 small bunch of **celery,** trimmed and sliced thin
½ lb. **brussels sprouts,** halved if large
1 **onion,** chopped
6 T. **butter**
2 **garlic** cloves, minced
¼ c. **flour**
4 c. **chicken broth**
1 tsp. **dried thyme**
1 c. **almond, rice,** *or* **coconut milk**
1 tsp. **Herbamare**
½ tsp. **black pepper**

*Serves 6*

*You can add a little almond, rice or coconut milk to make it creamy.*

1. Cook cauliflower, celery and brussells sprouts in a small amount of water, covered until tender.

2. In another pan, cook onion and butter over moderate heat, stirring for 4 minutes, add garlic and flour and cook 3 min.

3. Add broth, thyme and cooked veggies and simmer a few more minutes.

4. Puree in food processor in batches, return to pan, add milk, salt and pepper. Simmer 5 min.

## Black Bean Soup with Chili, Coconut Milk, and Lime

*Serves 4*

*One of my favorite quick meals. Delicious every time.*

---

2 T. extra-virgin **olive oil**
1 small **onion,** peeled and finely chopped
1 ½ tsp. **cumin**
1 tsp. ground **chipotle chili**
¼ cup **cilantro leaves,** plus extra for garnish
½ cup **water**
2 (15 oz.) cans **black beans,** undrained
1 (5.46 oz.) can **coconut milk**
1 tsp. **sea salt**
juice of 2 **limes**

---

1. Heat oil in soup pot over medium heat. Add onion, cumin, chili, and cilantro. Cook 5 minutes, stirring frequently.

2. Add water, lower heat and cook until onion is soft – about 10 - 12 minutes.

3. Add beans with liquid and coconut milk. Bring to a boil, lower heat and simmer for 15 minutes.

4. Remove from heat, add salt and lime juice. Ladle into bowls and garnish with cilantro.

# Chicken Entrees

*Company Roast Chicken (p.73)*

## Chicken Strognaoff

2 T. extra-light **olive oil**
1 lb. **ground chicken** *or* **turkey**
1 medium **onion,** chopped
1 clove **garlic,** minced or pressed
1 cup **chicken broth**
1 tsp. **Herbamare** *or* **sea salt**
¼ tsp. **black pepper**
1 tsp. **dried thyme**

*Serves 4*

*This is one of my favorite "quickies". It is simple, and delicious.*

*To make a deluxe stroganoff, add oregano, pine nuts, pesto and another can of chicken broth.*

1. Heat oil in large frying pan, and lightly brown chicken.

2. As chicken begins to brown, add onion and garlic, stirring until onion is limp.

3. Add broth and seasonings, and simmer a few minutes until thickened.

4. Serve over rice, millet, quinoa, garlic mashed potatoes or angel hair pasta.

## Chicken in Ginger Sauce

4 (6 oz.) boneless **chicken** *or* **turkey breasts,** skinned
2 T. light **olive oil**
6 **green onions,** finely chopped
3 **garlic** cloves, crushed
2" piece fresh **gingerroot,** peeled and finely minced
1 tsp. **cumin**
2 tsp. **garam masala**
**salt** and **black pepper** to taste
1 T. **lemon juice**
6 T. hot **water**

*Serves 4*

*This recipe also works well in a crockpot. Just put all ingredients in theß crockpot and cook on high for 3-4 hours.*

1. Rinse chicken, pat dry with paper towels, and slice thinly.

2. Heat oil in large skillet, add onions and cook 2 - 3 min. to soften,

stirring. Remove from pan with a slotted spoon.

3. Add chicken to pan and cook over med-high heat, stirring frequently, for about 5 min., or until browned.

4. Stir in garlic, gingerroot, cumin, garam masala, salt and pepper. Cook 1 min.

5. Stir in cooked onions, lemon juice, and water. Cover and cook over low heat about 10 min, or until chicken is tender. Pour sauce over chicken.

## Baked Rosemary Chicken

1 whole **chicken**
4 - 6 **lemons**
1 T. **olive oil**
2 T. **dried rosemary**
4 large cloves **garlic,** peeled
**Herbamare** and **black pepper** to taste.

*Serves 4*

1. Rinse chicken and pat dry with paper towels.

2. Rub skin with oil.

3. Cut lemons in quarter and insert garlic and lemons in chicken cavity.

4. Crumble rosemary inside and on skin of chicken.

5. Sprinkle Herbamare and pepper over chicken.

6. Bake at 425° 1 hour and 15 min., remove from oven.

7 Make gravy with juices, flour, chicken broth, salt and pepper.

## Company Roast Chicken

1 (4 lb.) whole organic **chicken**
1 whole head of **garlic,** cloves peeled
2 **lemons,** quartered

*Serves 4*

*You won't want to wait
for company to make
this again!*

**fresh thyme** (*or* **oregano** and **rosemary**—fresh if possible)
4 strips organic **turkey bacon**
½ stick melted **butter** with added sea salt and pepper
1 cup **chicken broth**
1 T. **Bragg's Liquid Aminos**
extra **lemon juice**

_____

1. Melt butter and add salt and pepper.

2. Liberally salt and pepper chicken inside and out.

3. Put lemons and garlic in chicken cavity, and place herbs on top.

4. Brush top with melted butter mixture.

5. Tie legs together with twine and place turkey bacon strips on top of chicken.

6. Bake in oven at 425* for 1 hour and 15 min.

7. Remove turkey bacon after 30 minutes, save, and cut up and add to a green salad later.

8. Remove chicken to a platter, remove twine, and make sauce by adding chicken broth, Bragg's Liquid Aminos and a little lemon juice to pan juices. Boil down to a sauce consistency.

9. Pour sauce over chicken and serve with garlic and lemon from the roast chicken.

## Barbecued Chicken

_____

*Serves 4*

*Garlic potatoes are
particularly good with
this dish.*

*Prepared spaghetti sauce
can be used in place of
tomato sauce, if yeast-free.*

**Chicken** pieces to serve 4
1 (8 oz.) can **tomato sauce**
¼ cup **Bragg's Liquid Aminos**
¼ cup **honey**
½ tsp. **black pepper**
1 tsp. **Roma, Pero,** *or* **other instant coffee substitute**
½ tsp. **Herbamare**

_____

1. Combine tomato sauce, Bragg's, honey, pepper, Roma, and Herbamare and pour over chicken.

2. Bake 1 hour at 400°, turning chicken over after 30 min.

3. Serve with plenty of sauce. .

## Spicy Chicken Patties

1 lb. ground **chicken** *or* **turkey**
4 **green onions,** finely chopped
2 **tomatoes,** peeled and chopped, opt.
3 T. chopped **cilantro**
1" piece fresh **gingerroot,** peeled and finely minced
1 large **garlic** clove, peeled and crushed
1 tsp. ground **cumin**
1 tsp. **garam masala**
1 tsp. **sea salt** and **cayenne pepper** to taste
1 **egg,** beaten
¼ cup light **olive oil**

*Serves 4*
*Divinely delicious.*

1. In a large bowl, mix together chicken, onions, tomatoes, cilantro, ginger-root, garlic, cumin, garam masala, salt, cayenne, and egg.

2. Roll into 4 patties, and cook in heated oil 4 - 6 min. on each side, until crisp and golden brown and no longer pink in center.

## Sausage, White Bean, and Pasta Chili

1 T. extra-virgin **olive oil**
1 lb. **Italian turkey sausage,** casings removed
2 (14oz.) cans diced **tomatoes with green chilies**
2 tsp. **paprika**
1 T. ground **cumin**
1 (15oz.) can **navy beans,** rinsed and drained

*Serves 4-6*

⅔ cup **tiny pasta shells,** cooked
14 oz. **chicken broth**
**Herbamare** and **pepper** to taste

_____

1.  Heat oil in large skillet, add turkey sausage, breaking it up into small chunks as you stir, until lightly browned.

2   Pour off any excess fat.

3.  Add the tomatoes and their liquid, chicken broth, paprika and cumin.

4.  Bring to a boil, reduce heat and simmer, uncovered, for 25 min.

5.  Remove from heat, stir in beans and cooked pasta, mixing thoroughly.

6.  Season with Herbamare and pepper to taste.

7.  Reheat before serving.


## Cornish Hens with Raspberry Sauce

_____

4 **Cornish game hens**
2 T. **butter**
¼ cup **lime juice**
¾ tsp. **sea salt**
¾ tsp. **black pepper**
⅓ cup toasted **sesame seeds**
1 (10 oz.) jar **raspberry jelly** sweetened with honey

_____

1.  Rinse hens and pat dry with paper towels.

*Serves 4*      2.  Melt butter, add ½ of the lime juice, salt and pepper.

*Company fare for sure!*   3.  Brush hens inside and out with butter mixture.

4.  Roast uncovered for 1 hour and 15 min. at 350°.

5.  In a saucepan combine seeds, jelly, and rest of lime juice. Melt on low., Brush some over hens the last 5 min. of cooking.

6   Pass rest of sauce at the table.

## Dave's Fabulous Turkey Burgers

1 lb. lean **ground turkey**
⅓ cup chopped **fresh mint**
3 finely minced **scallions** with 3" green tops
⅓ cup **rice** or **soy parmesan cheese**
2 **garlic** cloves, crushed
½ tsp. **sea salt**
½ tsp. **black pepper**

*Serves 4*

*If you can't find parmesan substitutes use grated pecorino romano – it's made from sheep's milk and small amounts are okay.*

1. Combine all and form into 4 patties
2. Spray skillet or grill and cook until no pink remains.

## Laura's Lemoned Chicken

4 pieces **chicken breasts**—with skin and bone
½ stick melted **butter**
grated rind of 2 **lemons**
¼ cup fresh **lemon juice**
¼ cup extra-virgin **olive oil**
½ tsp. **sea salt**
½ tsp. freshly ground **black pepper** (important!)
1 tsp. **dried oregano**
hot **cooked rice**

*Serves 4*

*I love lemon and use it a lot. This recipe satisfies my craving.*

*If boned and skinned chicken breasts are used, cook only 45 min.*

1. Place chicken in greased casserole.
2. In small bowl, combine all other ingredients and pour over the chicken.
3. Bake 1 hour at 350°, basting every 20 minutes.
4. Cook rice according to package directions.
5. Remove chicken from casserole and boil juices down to a light sauce consistency.
6. Place rice and chicken on a platter and pour juices over all. .

# Grilled Lime Buttered Turkey Tenderloins

*Serves 4*

¼ cup **butter,** melted
¼ cup fresh **lime juice**
2 tsp. **dry mustard**
2 (¾ lb.) **turkey breast tenderloins**
1 tsp. **garlic powder**
**sea salt** and **pepper** to taste

1. Combine first 4 ingredients, divide in half and set aside.

2. Basting with half the marinade, grill the tenderloins over medium-hot coals, covered, turning once or twice, until the thermometer reaches 170°.

3. In a small saucepan, cook remaining marinade until thoroughly heated and pour over cooked tenderloins.

4. Add salt and pepper.

# Moroccan Lemon Chicken with Black Olives

*Serves 4*

1 medium **onion,** peeled and quartered
2 - 3 **garlic** cloves, peeled and minced
1 whole **chicken,** or chicken parts, skin removed
4 T. **flour**
2 T. extra-virgin **olive oil**
2 ½ cups **water,** divided
1 tsp. each: ground **ginger, cumin,** and **paprika**
½ tsp. **sea salt**
grated peel of 2 **lemons**
3 T. fresh **lemon juice**
½ cup sliced **black olives**
½ cup minced **cilantro**
freshly ground **black pepper** to taste
¾ cup **couscous**
½ tsp. **Herbamare**

1. In a food processor, finely chop onion and garlic.

2. Put flour and chicken in a paper bag and shake to coat.

3. In a large skillet, heat oil over medium heat, and saute chicken and onion mixture until onion is soft—about 10 minutes.

4. Stir in 1 cup water, ginger, cumin, paprika, salt and lemon peel. Bring to a boil, reduce heat and simmer, covered, 35 min.

5. Remove chicken from sauce to cool a few minutes.

6. Debone chicken and cut meat into small pieces. Put back into sauce with lemon juice, olives, cilantro, and pepper. Simmer 5 min.

7. While chicken is simmering, bring 1 ½ cups water and ½ tsp. Herbamare to a boil in a medium saucepan. Add the couscous and bring it back to a boil. Remove from heat and let sit covered for 5 min. Fluff with fork.

8. Spoon chicken mixture over couscous and serve.

## Caribbean Chicken Stew

2 T. light **olive oil**
1 large **yellow onion,** chopped
1 large **green pepper,** chopped
3 **garlic** cloves, crushed
2 tsp. **cinnamon**
1 tsp. each **allspice** and **nutmeg**
½ tsp. **cayenne pepper,** or to taste
1 T. **Herbamare**
1 tsp. **black pepper**
1 **bay leaf**
1 (16 oz.) can diced **tomatoes**
2 cups **chicken broth**
1 ½ lbs. **chicken breast/thighs,** poached and pulled into strips
1 ½ cups **winter squash,** cubed
1 (15.5 oz.) can **black beans,** undrained
4 **limes,** each cut into quarters

*Serves 6-8*

*Brimming with anti-oxidants and flavor.*

1   Heat oil in large pot. Add onion, green pepper,, and garlic and saute for 3 minutes.

2   Add tomatoes, broth, chicken, squash, and beans. Simmer covered 20 - 25 minutes, stirring occasionally.

3   Remove bay leaf. Serve over brown rice with juice from lime wedges.

## Oriental Chicken

*Serves 3-4*

*If whole breasts are used, bake 20 min. at 350°.*

1 lb. **chicken tenders,** or strips of chicken breasts
2 T. toasted **oriental sesame oil**
2 T. **Bragg's Liquid Aminos**
**garlic salt** to taste

1.  Pour sesame oil and Bragg's over chicken.

2.  Sprinkle with garlic salt to taste and let marinate for at least 3 hours.

3.  Saute strips in hot skillet just a few minutes or until done.

## Chicken with Lime Butter

*Serves 6*

2 lbs. **chicken tenders**
½ tsp. **sea salt**
½ tsp. **black pepper**
⅓ cup light **olive oil**
1 large **lime,** juiced
1 stick or 8 T. **butter**
1 tsp. minced **chives,** frozen or fresh
1 tsp. **dried dill weed**
**Jane's Crazy Mixed-Up Salt** to taste

1.  Sprinkle chicken on both sides with salt and pepper.

2.  In large skillet, heat oil to medium temperature. Saute chicken 3 min. or until light brown. Turn chicken, cover, reduce heat to low.

Cook 8 min. or until tender. Remove chicken and keep warm.

3. Discard oil, and in same pan cook lime juice on low heat until juice just begins to bubble.

4. Add butter and stir until sauce is blended and slightly thickened. Stir in chives, dill weed and Jane's, and spoon sauce over chicken. .

## Lemon-Dill Chicken

3 T. **butter**
1 T. **dried dill weed**
2 T. freshly squeezed **lemon juice**
1 tsp. **sea salt**
½ tsp. **paprika**
¼ tsp. **black pepper**
1 large clove **garlic,** minced
1 (3 lb.) **broiler-fryer,** cut up and skin removed
hot **cooked rice**

*Serves 4*

*This is sinfully easy and delicious.*

*Turkey tenderloins can be used in this recipe. Cook 35 min.*

1. Melt butter in a large skillet over medium heat.

2. Add dill weed, lemon juice, salt, paprika, pepper and garlic. Bring to a boil.

3. Add chicken pieces in a single layer, and return to a boil.

4. Cover, reduce heat and simmer 45 min. or until tender, turning once.

5. Serve over hot cooked rice, spooning sauce over all. .

## Citrus-Rosemary Turkey Breast

1 (3 - 4 lb.) bone-in **turkey breast**
2 T. **butter,** softened
2 large **garlic** cloves, minced
½ tsp. **sea salt** and **pepper**
1 **lemon,** thinly sliced
2 **fresh rosemary sprigs,** *or* 1 tsp. **dried rosemary**
2 **fresh sage leaves,** *or* 1 tsp. **dried sage**

*Serves 4*

½ tsp. **Herbamare**
1 cup **chicken broth** with one chopped **onion**

_____

1.  Stir together butter and garlic. Loosen skin from turkey without detaching it. Sprinkle salt and pepper under skin, rub garlic mixture over meat.

2.  Place lemon slices, rosemary, and sage under skin. Replace skin.

3.  Rub a little extra butter over skin and sprinkle with Herbamare, Place on lightly greased rack in a broiling pan. Add chicken broth and onion.

4.  Bake at 350° for 1 to 1 ½ hours, basting occasionally, until meat thermometer registers 170° to 180°. Let stand 10 min. before slicing. Serve with pan juices.

## Grilled Lemon and Herb Marinated Cornish Game Hens

*Serves 4-6*

*Hens may be broiled in oven 4" from heat, skin side down, turning once, for 20-25 min.*

2 tsp. **dried oregano**
2 tsp. **dried thyme**
2 tsp. **dried rosemary**
4 cloves **garlic,** minced
1 tsp. **sea salt**
3 **Cornish game hens,** halved, the backbones cut out and discarded, and patted dry
½ cup freshly squeezed **lemon juice**
¼ cup extra-virgin **olive oil**

_____

1.  Mix together the lemon juice, oil, oregano, thyme, rosemary, garlic and salt in a shallow baking dish large enough to hold the hens in one layer.

2.  Turn hens to coat them evenly with marinade. Cover and let them marinate and chill overnight if possible.

3.  Drain hens, reserving marinade, and grill them over glowing coals on a rack set 5 - 6" from heat.

4. Baste with marinade and turn hens several times. Cook 20 min. or until juices of the thigh run clear when pricked.

## Curried Chicken and Rice Salad

1 ½ cups cooked cubed **chicken**
1 ½ cups **cooked rice,** cooked in chicken broth
⅓ cup **onion,** diced
⅓ cup **green pepper,** chopped
1 cup **celery,** chopped
1 T. freshly squeezed **lemon juice**
2 T. extra-virgin **olive oil**
2 tsp. **curry powder**
¾ cup homemade **mayonnaise,** (p. 142)
1 tsp. **Herbamare**

*Serves 3-4*

*This is my "go to" recipe for chicken salad. Curry is a major anti-fungal seasoning.*

1. In a large bowl, toss together the chicken, rice, onion, green pepper, celery, lemon juice, oil and curry powder.

2. Refrigerate.

3. Just before serving add mayonnaise and Herbamare.

## Asian Chicken Salad

2 cups chopped cooked **chicken** *or* **turkey**
1 cup diced **red pepper**
5 sliced **scallions**
3 T. homemade **mayonnaise,** (p. 142)
1 T. **Bragg's Liquid Aminos**
2 tsp. **toasted sesame oil**

*Serves 3-4*

1. Mix mayonnaise, Bragg's, and sesame oil to make dressing.

2. Toss chicken, red pepper, and scallions.

3 Add dressing and refrigerate. .

## Craig's Quickie Spaghetti Sauce

*Serves 4*

*I always add 2 more T. extra-virgin olive oil before serving.*

2 T. extra-virgin **olive oil**
1 lb. **ground turkey**
1 can (26oz.) Hunt's **Garlic and Herb Spaghetti Sauce** (no sugar)
4 cloves **garlic,** chopped or pressed
1 tsp. ea. **dried rosemary, basil** and **oregano**
½ tsp. **sea salt** and **pepper** to taste

1.  Saute ground turkey in olive oil until no longer pink.

2.  Add garlic, sauce, herbs, salt/pepper. Cover, simmer 15 - 20 min.

3.  Spoon over hot pasta or spaghetti squash.

## Chicken Spaghetti Sauce

*Serves 4*

¼ cup extra-virgin **olive oil**
½ cup **onion,** chopped
2 cloves **garlic,** chopped
1 lb. uncooked **ground chicken** *or* **turkey**
1 tsp. **garlic powder**
1 T. dried **parsley flakes**
1 cup (or 8 oz.) **tomato sauce**
2 cups (or 1 lb. can) **tomatoes**
1 ½ tsp. **sea salt**
1 tsp. **dried oregano**
1 tsp. **dried basil**
¼ tsp. **black pepper**
1 **bay leaf**
1 lb. box **thin spaghetti**

1.  In large skillet, cook oil, onions, and garlic for 5 min.

2.  Stir in chicken and garlic powder and brown slightly.

3.  Add parsley, tomato sauce, tomatoes, salt, oregano, basil, pepper

and bay leaf. Cover and simmer for 1 hr.

4. Uncover and cook for 30 min. or until desired consistency.

5. Remove bay leaf and spoon over cooked spaghetti.

# Lasagne

---

1 lb. **spicy chicken** *or* **turkey sausage,** casings removed

3 cloves garlic, minced

1 tsp. **Jane's Crazy Mixed-Up Salt**

3 cups canned **tomatoes**

2 (6 oz.) cans Hunt's Italian **tomato paste**

1 T. **dried basil**

6 **lasagne noodles**

2 (10.5 oz.) Mori Nu soft **tofu**

½ cup **rice** *or* **almond milk cheese substitute** topping

2 T. **dried parsley**

1 **egg,** beaten

1 T. **Italian Seasoning**

1 tsp. **Jane's Crazy Mixed-Up Salt**

½ tsp. **black pepper**

1 lb. **rice** *or* **almond yeast-free mozzarella cheese substitute**

---

*Serves 8*

*Not like your mama used to make, but satisfying nonetheless.*

*Sometimes I add 2 C. spinach to the meat sauce 5 min. before it is through cooking.*

1. Brown meat slowly and spoon off excess fat.

2. Add next 5 ingredients and simmer uncovered 30 min, stirring occasionally.

3. Cook noodles in large amount of salted water until tender. Drain and rinse.

4. Combine remaining ingredients except mozzarella.

5. Place ½ noodles in a lightly oiled lasagne pan. Spread with ½ the tofu mixture, ½ mozzarella and ½ the meat sauce.

6. Repeat layers.

7. Bake at 375° 40 - 45 min.

8. Let stand 10 min. before cutting.

# Chinese Hot Chicken Salad

*Serves 8*

*Wonderful for luncheons
as well as dinner*

*Leftover chicken or
turkey can be used also.*

2 whole bone-in **chicken breasts** (1 ¾ lb.)
6 cups shredded **romaine lettuce**
1 (8 oz.) can sliced **water chestnuts,** drained
2 medium **carrots,** peeled and coarsely shredded
¼ cup **Bragg's Liquid Aminos**
2 T. **honey**
1 large **garlic** clove, minced
3 T. **chicken broth**
2 tsp. light **olive oil**
¾ cup finely chopped **scallions**
2 tsp. peeled and finely chopped **ginger root**
¼ tsp. coarsely chopped **black pepper**
¼ tsp. crushed **hot pepper flakes**

1. Split chicken breasts in half, place in large saucepan. Cover with water and bring to a simmer over medium heat.

2. Reduce to low, cover and simmer 15 min. Remove from heat and let stand, covered for 20 min.

3. Remove chicken from broth and discard skin, bones and fat. Cut chicken into 1 inch strips.

4. Toss together the lettuce, water chestnuts and carrots. Arrange on a large serving platter. Top with chicken shreds.

5. In a small bowl, combine the Bragg's, honey and garlic. Stir to mix well. In a small saucepan, combine chicken broth, oil, scallions, ginger, cracked pepper and hot pepper. Bring to a simmer over low heat, about 3 min.

6. Stir in Bragg's mixture and pour sauce over chicken. Serve at once.

# Goat Cheese-Stuffed Chicken

¼ cup **walnuts**
¼ cup fresh **goat cheese,** softened

½ - 1 tsp. freshly grated **lemon zest**
1 large **garlic** clove, minced
sea salt and freshly **ground pepper**
4 skinless, boneless **chicken breast halves**
1 T. extra-virgin **olive oil**
3 T. fresh **lemon juice**
¼ cup **chicken broth**
2 T. **walnut oil** (no substitutes!)
¼ cup chopped **flat leaf parsley** *or* **cilantro**

*Serves 4*

*After 21 days small amounts of goat cheese can be added to the diet.*

*This is a wonderful recipe to reward yourself with. I love to make this for company.*

1. Preheat oven to 400*. Spread the walnuts in a pie plate and toast for 6 min. Let cool, then chop.

2. In a small bowl, mash the goat cheese with the lemon zest, garlic, and half the chopped walnuts; season with salt and pepper.

3. Using a small knife, cut a pocket in the side of each chicken breast, keeping the opening as small as possible. Stuff the chicken breasts with the mixture and use a rolling pen to flatten slightly.

4. In a large, oven-proof skillet, heat the olive oil until shimmering. Season the chicken with salt and pepper and cook over moderately high heat, turning once, until browned— around 3 minutes each side.

5. Transfer the skillet to the oven (still at 400*) and cook chicken for 5 min. Transfer chicken to a platter and keep warm.

6. Add the lemon juice and broth to the skillet, and cook over moderately high heat, scraping up any browned bits stuck to the pan. Simmer for 3 min. the stir in walnut oil, parsley and the remaining chopped walnuts.

7. Transfer the chicken breasts to plates and spoon the walnut sauce on top and serve.

## Chicken Fingers

2 cups **almond flour**
2 tsp. **smoked paprika**

1 ½ tsp. **garlic salt**
1 tsp. **dry mustard**
½ tsp. **black pepper**
1 **egg**
1 ½ lb. **chicken tenders**

---

1. Preheat oven to 475*. Line two baking sheets with unbleached parchment paper. Set a wire rack on each and spray with cooking spray.

2. Mix almond flour, paprika, dry mustard, garlic salt and pepper in a bowl.

3. Whisk egg and coat chicken tenders well on both sides.

4. Toss with almond mixture, coating evenly.

5. Place on wire racks and cook 20 - 25 minutes until golden brown.

## Avocado Chicken Salad

---

2 cups shredded, cooked **chicken**
1 **avocado**
1 tsp. **garlic powder**
¾ tsp. **sea salt**
¾ tsp. **pepper**
1 T. **lime juice**
⅓ cup **homemade mayonnaise**, (p. 142)
⅓ cup canned **coconut milk**

---

1. Mix together lightly and chill.

# Fish Entrees

Please buy only wild-caught fish if possible. Farm-raised fish are fed genetically modified corn (fish don't eat corn!), swim in feces- and antibiotic-laced water, and are very prone to disease. Their omega 3:6 ratio is decidedly unfavorable as farm-raised fish contain up to 400 percent more omega 6 fatty acids than wild caught fish, creating an unhealthy imbalance that contributes to inflammation in the body. The flesh of farm-raised salmon is grey, so artificial color has to be added to make them look normal and pink. In the grocery store and eating out, always ask for wild-caught fish.

## Fabulous Fish Soup

*Serves 8*

*I have a friend who loved this so much the first time she made it three nights in a row!*

7 **carrots,** sliced thin
6 ribs of **celery** and tops, sliced thin
3 boiling **potatoes,** peeled and cut into l" cube
2 **onions,** chopped
½ cup extra-virgin **olive oil**
1 (l6 oz. can) **stewed tomatoes**
2 qts. **water,** *or* **chicken broth**
1 T. **Herbamare**
1 tsp. freshly **ground pepper**
1 ½ lb. **orange roughy,** cut into bite-sized pieces
1 T. **dried dill weed**
1 T. **dried tarragon**
1 bunch **cilantro,** chopped

1.  In a large pot heat the oil, add carrots, celery, potatoes and onions and saute for 5 min.

2.  Add tomatoes, water, and simmer mixture for 20 min., or until vegetables are tender.

3.  Add the fish, Herbamare, pepper, dill and tarragon, and cook at a bare simmer for 20 min.

4.  Add chopped cilantro a few minutes before serving.

## Almond Shrimp and Peppers

*Serves 4*

1 ½ lb. medium **shrimp,** peeled
3 T. **lemon juice,** divided
3 cloves **garlic**
⅛ tsp. **red pepper flakes**
½ tsp. **black pepper**
1 T. extra-virgin **olive oil.**
¾ cup blanched **slivered almonds**
4 T. **butter,** divided
1 **red bell pepper**
2 T. **fresh** *or* 2 tsp. **dried chives**

2 T. chopped **fresh parsley**
2 tsp. **dried basil**
½ tsp. **sea salt**

1. Combine 2 T. lemon juice with garlic, red pepper flakes, pepper, oil. Marinate shrimp in mixture for 15 minutes.
2. Saute almonds in 2 T. butter until golden.
3. Add shrimp and red bell pepper. Saute 2 - 3 min. Remove from heat.
4. Stir in herbs, salt, 1 T. lemon juice, and 2 T. butter. Serve over rice.

## Sauteed Monkfish

1 - 1 ½ lb. **monkfish**, grey skin removed
3 T. light **olive oil**
2 tsp. **dried oregano**
**white flour** for dredging
1 - 2 **eggs**
**garlic powder** (opt.) to taste
**Herbamare** to taste

*Serves 4*

*Monkfish is called "the poor man's lobster." It has the look, feel, and taste of lobster at half the price. Delicious. Don't overcook.*

1. Cut monkfish into small medallions (1 - 2 inch cubes).
2. .Combine flour, oregano, garlic powder and Herbamare.
3. Beat eggs well, dip fish pieces in the egg, then roll in seasoned flour.
4. Heat iron skillet over medium heat, add olive oil, and saute gently 3 - 4 min. each side until fish is done.

## Aegean Shrimp

1 **onion,** chopped
½ cup extra-virgin **olive oil**
2 medium **tomatoes**
2 **garlic** cloves, crushed
1 small **bay leaf**

½ tsp. **dried basil**
1 tsp. **dried oregano**
¼ cup chopped **fresh parsley**
½ tsp. **hot sesame oil** (do NOT omit)
**sea salt** and freshly ground **black pepper** to taste
1 lb. fresh **shrimp,** peeled
½ lb. **feta cheese,** crumbled (from sheep)
8 or more **black olives,** halved
½ **lemon**

_Serves 4-5_
_This recipe is allowed_
_only in the third month,_
_when your body can_
_handle small amounts of_
_feta. Make sure the feta_
_you get is sheep's milk_
_and not cow's._

1. In a large skillet over medium-high heat, saute onion in olive oil until soft.

2. Add tomatoes, garlic, bay leaf, basil, oregano, parsley, hot sesame oil, salt and pepper. Cook 4 - 5 min.

3. Remove vegetables from skillet with a slotted spoon, leaving juices in skillet, and spread vegetables in bottom of a 2 qt. casserole.

4. Bring pan juices to a boil, add shrimp and cook 2 min.

5. Add shrimp mixture to casserole, crumble feta over top.

6. Arrange olives on top of feta, and squeeze lemon over all.

7. Bake in pre-heated 375° oven 10 - 15 min. Serve over rice. .

## Shrimp and Rice Salad

1 cup **basmati rice**
6 T. extra-virgin **olive oil**
1 lb. **shrimp,** shelled and deveined
3 T. fresh **lime juice**
2 large cloves **garlic,** minced or pressed
½ cup minced **cilantro leaves**
rind of 1 **lime,** grated
**salt** _and_ **pepper** to taste

_Serves 4_
_Canned salmon can be_
_substituted for shrimp_
_if you like._

1. Cook rice in 2 c. water, 1 tsp. salt for 20 min.

2. In heavy skillet heat 2 T. oil until hot but not smoking. Stir-fry

shrimp until cooked through (1 - 3 minutes). Remove from heat and stir in lime juice and garlic.

3. In a bowl, stir together the rice, shrimp, remaining oil, rind, cilantro, and salt and pepper to taste.

## Seared Tuna Salad

---

4 serving pieces of **fresh tuna** from the loin
4 T. extra-virgin **olive oil**
1 tsp. **sea salt** *and* ½ tsp. **pepper**
Zest of one large **lime**
1 tsp. **wasabi powder**
⅓ cup fresh **lime juice**
2 T. **Bragg's Liquid Aminos**
Big pinch of **cayenne pepper**
Chopped **red onion** *and* chopped **scallions**
2 sliced **avocados**
**Mixed salad greens**

---

*Serves 4*

*One of my favorite recipes.*

*Be sure to use fresh high grade tuna. Cook tuna only one-fourth the way up the filet on each side. Middle half should remain pinkish.*

1. Brush tuna well with olive oil and salt and pepper, Sear tuna 2 min. or less on each side. Remove to plate.

2. Make dressing by mixing together the olive oil, sea salt and pepper, lime zest, wasabi powder, lime juice, Bragg's Liquid Aminos and cayenne.

3. Dice tuna and put over mixed greens.

4. Add chopped onions, scallions and sliced avocados.

5. Pour dressing over all.

## Fish Baked in Parchment Paper

---

1 ¼ lbs. **fish,** such as cod, tilapia, mahi-mahi, orange roughy, etc.
4 inch piece **fresh ginger,** peeled and cut into matchsticks
6 **scallions,** chopped

*Serves 4*

2 **garlic cloves,** finely chopped
2 T. **Bragg's Liquid Aminos**
1 T. fresh **lemon juice**
1 tsp. **toasted sesame oil**
1 tsp. **red pepper flakes**

_____

1. Arrange four fish fillets in center of its own large square of parc
   ment paper. Scatter over the ginger, scallions and garlic.
2. Drizzle each piece with Bragg's, lemon, sesame oil and pepper flakes.
   Pull corners of parchment paper together to form a tent and secure
   with string.
3. Place bundles on a baking sheet and bake 20 min. at 400°. Serve as
   is or remove fish and juices to warmed plates.

## Herb and Garlic Fish

_____

*Serves 4*

*Also good with a mixture of mayonnaise, lemon juice, thyme, tarragon and Herbamare.*

1 lb. **fish fillets**
½ cup **homemade mayonnaise,** (p. 142)
½ tsp. **dried marjoram**
½ tsp. **dried thyme**
½ tsp. **garlic powder**
½ tsp. **celery salt**

_____

1. Mix mayonnaise and seasonings.
2. Place fish in greased casserole, and brush with mixture.
3. Bake 15 - 20 min. at 350°.

## Sylvia's Seviche

_____

1 lb. **shrimp**
**celery tops, green onion tops,**

1 large **garlic**
½ **purple onion**
2 **tomatoes**, chopped
1 cup **cilantro**, chopped
½ cup **parsley**, chopped
¼ - ½ cup **homemade ketchup** (p. 144)
2 **garlic** cloves, chopped
1 **orange**, in sections
2 T. **lemon juice**

*Serves 4*

*Traditionally served with popcorn in South America.*

1. Cook shrimp in 6 cups water with celery tops, green onion tops, and garlic for 1 min. Let cool in water. Peel.
2. Slice purple onion and pour a little hot water over it to soften. Let cool. Drain.
3. Mix all together and chill thoroughly.

## Fish with Cilantro Ginger Sauce

1 lb. **fish fillets**, such as bass, cod, grouper, or orange roughy
1 T. fresh **gingerroot**, peeled and slivered
2 cloves **garlic**, chopped
¼ cup chopped **fresh cilantro**
¼ cup extra-virgin **olive oil**
2 T. fresh **lime juice**
dash **sea salt**
¼ tsp. freshly ground **black pepper**

*Serves 3-4*

1. Wash fish, pat dry, and place in a 9" x 12" glass baking dish.
2. Process ginger and garlic in food processor until finely chopped.
3. Add cilantro, oil, lime juice, salt to taste and pepper. Process about 2 min.
4. Pour marinade over fish and let stand at room temperature about 15 min.
5. Bake at 450° on lower rack 10 - 12 min.

## Sesame Crusted Sea Bass

*Serves 4*

*This is wonderful on other fishes as well.*

1 lb **sea bass** filets
1 T. dark, **toasted sesame oil**
3 T. lightly **toasted sesame seeds, salt** *and* **pepper** to taste

1.  Rub fish all over with sesame oil. Season with salt and pepper.

2.  Place in lightly oiled casserole and sprinkle both sides with seeds.

3.  Bake at 350° 20 min. or until done.


## Sophie's Salmon Burgers

*Serves 4*

1 (14.75 oz.) can **salmon**, pink or red, drained and skin removed
1 medium **potato,** peeled and boiled
1 T. **Bragg's Liquid Aminos**
2 tsp. **fresh ginger,** peeled and grated
2 **garlic** cloves, crushed
½ tsp. **black pepper**

1.  Mash salmon and potato. Mix in Bragg's, ginger, garlic, salt and pepper.

2.  Form into 4 patties. Spray skillet or grill with olive oil and cook on each side for four min.


## Salmon and Potato Salad

*Serves 4*

1 (7 oz.) can **salmon**, drained and flaked
¼ cup **cilantro**, chopped
1 large clove **garlic**, minced
¾ cup **homemade mayonnaise** (p. 142)
⅓ cup **celery,** diced

⅓ cup **red onion,** diced
1 lb. **red potatoes,** cooked and quartered with skin left on
**sea salt** *and* **pepper** to taste

_____

1. Place mayonnaise, cilantro, garlic, red onion and celery into a large mixing bowl. Combine well.

2. Add salmon and potatoes, gently mixing all ingredients to coat.

3. Salt and pepper to taste. Chill 1 - 3 hours.

## Poached Salmon Steaks

_____

4 **salmon steaks**
**water** to cover
½ tsp. **sea salt**
chopped **celery tops**
chopped **green onions** plus tops
½ cup **homemade mayonnaise** (p. 142)
2 T. **green onions** *or* **fresh** *or* **frozen chives**
1 tsp. **lemon juice**
1 tsp. **dried tarragon**
1 tsp. **dried dill weed**
¼ tsp. **Herbamare**

_____

*Serves 4*

*Tender and melt in your mouth. Spoon bread and slaw are perfect here.*

1. Place salmon steaks in a skillet, add water to cover, with celery tops, green onions and sea salt.

2. Bring to boiling point, cover, reduce heat to low, and simmer 5 minutes. Remove from heat and place fish on a platter.

3. Mix mayonnaise, onions or chives, lemon juice, tarragon, dill weed and Herbamare.

4. Put sauce on top of each steak and serve immediately. .

## Simple Tuna Salad

*Serves 4*

2 (6 oz.) cans **tuna** packed in water
½ cup **homemade mayonnaise** (p. 142)
3 **celery** stalks, chopped
¼ cup **green onions,** chopped
¼ cup **green pepper,** chopped
1 cup chopped **cilantro**
**Herbamare** to taste

1. Toss all together, and refrigerate.

## Crab or Salmon Stuffed Potatoes

*Serves 4*

*These freeze nicely.*

*Be careful. Unfortunately some manufacturers have started adding yeast extract to cheese substitutes to add flavor, a real no-no. Read labels like a hawk.*

*In a pinch you can use pecorino romano.*

4 baking **potatoes**
½ cup **butter**
¼ cup **almond milk**
1 tsp. **Herbamare**
½ tsp. **black pepper**
½ cup chopped **green onion**
1 **jalapeno,** seeded and chopped
1 cup **almond milk cheddar** *or* **jack style cheese**
1 cup fresh **crabmeat,** *or* two 6 oz. cans **pink salmon**
½ tsp. **paprika**

1. Bake potatoes at 400° 1 hour or until tender.
2. Cut potatoes in half, scoop out potato and mix with butter, milk, Herbamare, pepper, green onion, cheese, and crabmeat.
3. Refill shells, sprinkle with paprika, and bake at 425° 15 min.

## Spicy Catfish

1 ½ lbs. **catfish**
1 T. light **olive oil**

2 cloves **garlic,** minced
1 T. **whole fennel seed** (do not omit)
1 tsp. **black pepper**
½ tsp. **sea salt**
¾ tsp. **paprika**
½ tsp. ground **thyme**
1 tsp. **dried basil**
1 tsp. **dried oregano**
2 T. fresh **lemon juice**

1. Put oil in bottom of large baking dish.

2. Place fish in dish in a single row.

3. Sprinkle garlic and all herbs over fish. Top with lemon juice.

4. Bake at 350° for 20 minutes or until done.

## Baked Fish with Chermoula Sauce

1 ½ lbs. **firm white fish fillets,** such as halibut or cod
**sea salt** *and* freshly **ground pepper**
1 cup **chermoula sauce** (below)
2 cups **cilantro leaves**
1 ½ cups **parsley leaves**
4 **garlic clove**s
¾ tsp. **sea salt**
2 tsp. **cumin seeds**
½ tsp. **coriander seeds**
1 tsp. **paprika**
⅛ tsp, **cayenne pepper**
⅓ - ½ cup extra-virgin **olive oil**
¼ cup freshly squeezed lemon juice

1. In a small skillet toast the cumin and coriander seeds lightly. Cool. Then grind in an electric coffee grinder.

2. Place cilantro, parsley, salt and garlic in food processor and process well

3. Add the ground seeds, paprika, cayenne pepper and lemon juice and process lightly.

*Serves 4*

*Tilapia, orange roughy, cod, sole, swordfish, etc. are equally good.*

*Serves 4*

*Chermoula is a pungent Moroccan herb sauce traditionally served with grilled fish. It's also great with roasted vegetables, lamb or chicken. All the ingredients are power-fully anti-fungal.*

4. While machine is still running slowly add olive oil.

5. Taste and adjust seasoning. Add more olive oil or salt if desired.

6. Season the fish with salt and pepper and place in an oiled baking dish. With a spatula place half the chermoula sauce over fish to coat well.

7. Refrigerate for 30 min. to allow flavors to infuse the fish. Then bake at 350* 20 min. or until it is opaque and flakes easily.

8. Using a spatula, transfer the fish to a platter of individual plates. Tip the juices in the pan over the fish.

9. Pass the remaining chermoula sauce at the table with lemon wedges.

## Slow Roasted Salmon

---

4 portions of **wild caught salmon** or one fillet to serve 4
Extra-virgin **olive oil**
**zest of two lemons**
**sea salt** *and* **black pepper**
2 T. **dried dill**

---

*Serves 4*

*This is my favorite way to cook fresh salmon.*

*Salmon can sit at room temperature for several hours, which makes it ideal for luncheons and picnics.*

1. Preheat oven to 200* and place a glass baking dish of hot water on bottom rack of oven to keep salmon moist while cooking.

2. Prepare a baking dish by coating it with olive oil, or place parcment paper in pan and coat with olive oil.

3. Lightly coat salmon with olive oil and sea salt and black pepper. Place skin side down in pan.

4. Top with lemon zest and dried dill.

5. Roast the salmon, checking frequently, 30 –45 minute depending on the thickness of the salmon. It should just be beginning to flake and juices will be forming on the surface when done. Remove skin and serve.

# Lamb Entrees

*"He tends his flock like
a shepherd. He gathers
the lambs in his arms
and carries them   close
to his heart,"*

ISAIAH 40:11

# Herbed Roast Leg of Lamb

*Serves 6*

*Lamb was the festival meat in biblical times. Unlike beef, the cell of lamb meat is small and easy to digest. Full of vitamins and minerals to nourish your body. A true physical and spiritual food.*

*A small, rolled and boned leg of lamb with the same seasonings cooks beautifully in a crock pot on low for 6-8 hours.*

1 (5 - 6 lb.) **leg of lamb**
8 - 10 cloves of **garlic**
2 - 4 T. **dried rosemary**
fresh **lemon juice**
**sea salt** *and* **black pepper**
1 can yeast-free **beef broth** *or* **bouillon**
(or use ¼ c. Bragg's mixed in ¾ c. water)
2 T. **flour**
**sea salt** *and* **black pepper** to taste

1. Make sure the butcher has removed the musk gland.

2. Remove as much excess fat as possible from the leg.

3. Peel garlic cloves and cut each into slivers. With a sharp knife make slits in the meat and insert garlic deep into the slits.

4. Crumble rosemary over the meat, sprinkle with lemon, salt and pepper.

5. Bake at 350° until meat thermometer reaches 140° - 145° at the deepest point. Center of lamb should be pinkish.

6. De-grease lamb juice, add flour and cook 1 minute. Add bouillon and cook until thickened. Season with salt and pepper.

# Broiled Lamb Chops

*Serves 4*

4 **lamb chops,** rib or loin
extra-virgin **olive oil**
4 - 6 large cloves **garlic**
1 T. **dried basil**
1 T. **dried marjoram**
**sea salt** *and* **black pepper** to taste
**lemon juice**

1. Two hours before cooking, rub chops with oil on both sides.

2. Crush garlic and rub into chops.

3. Combine basil and marjoram and rub into meat.

4. Sprinkle lemon juice and salt and pepper over meat.

5. Cover and refrigerate until ready to broil.

6. Broil on a rack about 2" from heat in a very hot pre-heated oven, 3 - 5 min. on each side. The center of the chops should remain pinkish.

## Lamb Patties

1 lb. **ground lamb**
½ tsp. **dried oregano**
½ tsp. **dried sage**
½ tsp. **dried thyme**
1 clove **garlic**, finely minced
½ tsp. **Herbamare**
¼ tsp. **black pepper**

*Serves 4*

*These make a good breakfast sausage, too.*

1. Mix spices into meat and shape into patties.

2. Broil or pan fry to taste.

3. Freeze any left over at once.

## Lamb and Rice Salad

1 cup uncooked **brown rice**
1 lb. **ground lamb**
3 medium-sized **tomatoes**, cut in ¼" dice
¼ cup chopped pitted **black olives**
½ cup chopped **cilantro**
4 T. chopped **fresh mint**
½ tsp. **cinnamon**
1 tsp. **Herbamare**
¼ tsp. **black pepper**
2 T. extra-virgin **olive oil**
2 medium sized **onions**, chopped
1 T. minced fresh **garlic**

*Serves 6*

*Do not make this recipe until the third month. By that time you should be able to tolerate small amounts of feta. Make sure it's sheep's milk feta.*

1 large **zucchini**, sliced
¼ cup **chicken broth**, if needed
½ cup coarsely crumbled **feta cheese**

___

1.  Cook rice in 2 ½ cups chicken broth or salted water until done. Set aside.

2.  In a large skillet, saute lamb over medium heat until browned through. Drain off fat, and set aside.

3.  Place tomatoes and their juices, olives, cilantro, mint, cinnamon, Herbamare and pepper in a large oven-proof casserole.

4.  Heat olive oil in a skillet over medium-high heat. Add onions, garlic, and zucchini. Saute, stirring occasionally for 10 min. or until vegetables are soft.

5.  Add rice, lamb and zucchini mixture to the casserole. Fold all ingredients together well. If mixture seems too dry, add chicken broth to moisten.

6.  Sprinkle feta cheese over top.

7.  Serve at room temperature, or to serve hot, bake at 350°, loosely covered, for 15 minutes.

## Lamb Loaf
___

1 lb. **ground lamb**
1 (8 oz.) can **tomato sauce**, *or* canned **tomatoes**
½ cup chopped **onion**
½ cup chopped **green pepper**
2 - 3 cloves **garlic**, chopped
1 tsp. **Herbamare**
½ tsp. **black pepper**
1 **egg**

___

*Serves 4*

*This is a staple in our house. It is wonderful left-over, and makes a killer sandwich on toasted yeast-free sourdough bread.*

1.  Mix all ingredients together lightly; place in greased loaf pan.

2.  Bake at 350° 1 hour. Drain well.

## Crock Pot Lamb Shanks

4 meaty **lamb shanks**
**garlic powder**
**Herbamare** Seasoning
**Trocomare** Seasoning
1 T. each **dried basil, marjoram, rosemary**
fresh **lemon juice**

1. Put lamb shanks in crock pot.

2. Squeeze fresh lemon juice over meat.

3. Cover shanks liberally with all seasonings.

4. Cover and cook on low 6 - 8 hours.

5, Serve with rice or garlic potatoes.

*Serves 4*

*Chicken thighs can be cook this way and are just as good! I also love to cook lamb chops (2 per person) using this recipe cooking 5-6 hours on low.*

## Lamb, Rice and Lentil Stew

1 lb. **ground lamb**
1 T. extra-virgin **olive oil**
1 large **onion,** chopped
5 - 6 cups **water,** divided
1 cup **lentils**
1 cup uncooked **rice**
3 tsp. **Herbamare**
¼ tsp. **black pepper**
2 tsp. **cumin**
1 bunch **cilantro**

*Serves 4*

*Leftover leg of lamb can be used instead of ground lamb. Just add near the end of cooking time.*

1. Brown lamb and onions in olive oil. Drain fat.

2. Add 3 cups of the water and add lentils. Cover and cook 15 min.

3. Add remaining water, rice, Herbamare, pepper and cumin. Bring to a boil, cover and cook until rice is done.

4. A few minutes before stew is done, add one bunch of chopped cilantro.

## Lamb Meatballs

---

1 lb. **ground lamb**
1 T. **dried oregano**
1 tsp. **dried basil**
1 T. ground **cinnamon**
3 - 4 cloves **garlic**, diced and 1 tsp. **sea salt**
3 T. fresh **flat parsley**, finely minced

---

1. Preheat oven to 375°

2. Mix all ingredients in a large bowl. Form into small meatballs and arrange in a greased baking dish.

3. Bake the meatballs for 15 - 20 min. Drain off any fat.

4. Serve with vegetables and brown rice.

## Lamb Stew

---

*Serves 4-6*

*Good on hot cooked noodles, rice, or mashed potatoes.*

1 ½ lbs. boneless **lamb shoulder,** *or* **leg**, cubed
2 T. **olive oil**
2 **tomatoes,** peeled and chopped
1 each: **yellow squash, zucchini, turnip**
1 cup cubed **potato**
½ cup each: **carrots, green pepper, onion, corn**
1 tsp. **garlic powder**
1 tsp. **thyme**
2 tsp. **Herbamare**
1 small **bay leaf**
2 cups **water**
½ bunch **cilantro**
¼ cup **flour**
2 T. **butter**

---

1. Heat oil in dutch oven and brown meat on all sides.

2. Add tomatoes, squash, zucchini, turnip, potato, carrots, green pepper, onion, corn, garlic powder, thyme, Herbamare, bay leaf

and water. Bring to boiling point, turn to low, cover and cook 1 ½ hours.

3.  Blend flour and butter and shape into small balls. Drop into simmering stew.

4.  Add chopped cilantro, cover and cook 5 - 10 more min. stirring several times. Remove bay leaf

## Spicy Braised Lamb with Sweet Potatoes

1 ½ lbs. **lamb** cut into chunks. (I use leg of lamb.)
2 **sweet potatoes** (about 1 pound)
1 (28 oz.) can whole peeled **tomatoes**
1 large **red onion** cut into wedges
1 T. ground **cumin**
1 T. ground **ginger**
1 tsp. ground **cinnamon**
½ tsp. **cayenne**
1 tsp. **sea salt**
½ cup **water**
1 (10 oz.) box plain **couscous** (don't use kind with hydrolyzed yeast protein)
2 cups **baby spinach**
**Herbamare** *and* **pepper** to taste

*Serves 4-5*

1.  Peel sweet potatoes and cut into ½ inch thick half-moons.

2.  In a 4 to 6 quart crock pot, combine the lamb, potatoes, tomatoes (with liquid), onion, cumin, ginger, cinnamon, cayenne, salt, and water.

3.  Cover and cook until meat is tender, on high for 4 - 5 hours, or on low for 7 - 8 hours.

4.  Ten minutes before serving, prepare the couscous according to package directions.

5.  Stir in spinach and cook 2 - 3 minutes.

6.  Ladle stew over couscous in bowls.

# Lamb Burgers on the Grill

---

*Serves 4*

*Yeast-free tortillas can be used also.*

1 lb. **ground lamb**
1 cup chopped **onion**
3 cloves **garlic,** chopped
1 tsp. **Herbamare**
½ cup. **homemade mayonnaise** (p. 142)
½ tsp. **wasabi powder**
1 tsp. **Bragg's Liquid Aminos**
Yeast-free sourdough **bread** for buns
Fresh **tomatoes** *and* **lettuce**
Bubbie's vinegar-free Kosher **Dill Pickles**

---

1. Mix lamb, onions, garlic and Herbamare into patties.

2. Grill a few minutes on each side, but leave middle pinkish.

3. Mix the mayonnaise, wasabi powder and Bragg's in a small bowl.

4. Spread on sourdough bread and add sliced tomatoes, lettuce and Bubbie's kosher dill pickles.


# Lamb Stuffed Grape Leaves

---

*Serves 8*

1 (16 oz.) jar of **grape leaves**
2 lbs. **ground lamb**
1 cup uncooked **rice,** washed and drained
freshly ground **black pepper** to taste
2 tsp. **dried thyme**
1 tsp. **dried oregano**
1 small **onion,** finely chopped
2 T. **butter**
3 large **onions,** sliced
1 quart canned **tomatoes**
1 quart **tomato sauce**

---

1. Wash grape leaves thoroughly to remove salt and/or vinegar.

2. Mix lamb with rice, pepper, thyme, oregano, and chopped onion.

3. In a large pan or Dutch oven, heat the butter, add the sliced onions and cook until transparent.

4. Add canned tomatoes and heat.

5 Stuff the grapes leaves (not too tightly) with the meat mixture, using about 1 T. of the mixture for each leaf. Shape each into a neat bundle and place in tomato-onion mixture.

6. Heat the tomato sauce and pour over the top.

7. Cover and simmer for one hour.

# Lamb Spaghetti Sauce

2 T. **olive oil**
½ cup **onion,** chopped
2 cloves **garlic,** minced
1 pound **ground lamb**
1 tsp. Santay **garlic powder**
2 T. **Italian herbs**
1 ½ tsp. **sea salt**
¼ tsp. **black pepper**
1 **bay leaf**
1 cup **tomato sauce**
1 (16 oz.) can **tomatoes**

*Serves 4*

*I love to put this on spaghetti squash to cut down on carbs. Good on cooked zucchini and cooked chopped cabbage too.*

1. Heat oil in skillet. Saute onion and garlic lightly.

2. Add ground lamb and garlic powder. Saute until no longer pink. Drain fat.

3. Add Italian herbs, salt, black pepper and bay leaf.

4. Add tomato sauce and canned tomatoes. Cover and simmer 15 - 20 minutes.

5. Uncover and cook a few more minutes until thickened to desired consistency.

6, Remove bay leaf.

7. Serve on hot pasta.

# Lamb Chops with Cumin, Cardamom, and Lime

*Serves 4*

8 ¾" rib **lamb chops**
3 **garlic** cloves, finely chopped
¼ tsp. ground **cumin**
¼ tsp. ground **cardamom**
2 T. fresh **lime juice**
¾ tsp. **sea salt**
½ tsp. **black pepper**
2 tsp. extra-virgin **olive oil**

1. Whisk together garlic, cumin, cardamom, lime juice, salt, pepper and 2 tsp. olive oil. Place chops in bowl with marinade for 1 hour, turning occasionally.

2. Broil 3 - 4 minutes on each side or until slightly pink in the middle.

# Vegetables, Starches and Pastas

*"Better a meal of vegetables where there is love, than a fattened calf with hatred."*

—PROVERBS 15:17

# Ratatouille

*Serves 6*

*Eat eggplant often—it is a wonderful anti-fungal and anti-cancer food.*

*Good hot or cold.*

2 large **zucchini,** sliced
1 ½ lbs. **eggplant,** quartered and sliced
1 medium **onion,** thinly sliced
¼ cup extra-virgin **olive oil**
1 ½ cups skinned and coarsely chopped **tomatoes**
2 large **green peppers,** thinly sliced
1 large clove **garlic,** finely chopped
**Herbamare** *and* **black pepper** to taste

1. Sprinkle zucchini and eggplant with salt and let stand for about an hour. Rinse and pat dry with paper towel.

2. Cook onion in half the oil until transparent.

3. Add zucchini and cook without browning for about 10 min.

4. Meanwhile, saute eggplant in remaining oil in a separate pan, turning slices over from time to time until just beginning to color.

5. Add tomatoes to onion and zucchini. When tomatoes have cooked down to a pulp, add green pepper, cooked eggplant and garlic.

6. Season and simmer gently for 1 hour, or until ratatouille has thickened.

# Sweet Pepper Saute

*Serves 4*

*This recipe is good with almost any meat or pasta dish.*

*If you want to serve this cold, add the juice of half a lemon, and add a little more olive oil, salt and pepper.*

1 large **sweet red pepper,** seeded and cut into strips
1 large **yellow pepper,** seeded and cut into strips
1 large **green pepper,** seeded and cut into strips
2 cloves **garlic,** cut in half
2 T. extra-virgin **olive oil**
**Herbamare** *and* **black pepper** to taste

1. Heat the oil in a large skillet.

2. Saute peppers and garlic until peppers are slightly softened.

3. Season with Herbamare and pepper to taste.

# Oriental Spinach

*Serves 4*

1 lb. fresh **spinach**
2 T. **butter**
1 T. finely minced **onion**
2 T. **sesame seeds**
2 T. **Bragg's Liquid Aminos**

1. Wash spinach well in cool water. Drain and remove stems.

2. Heat butter in a skillet. Add onions and sesame seeds, cooking and stirring over medium heat until seeds are brown.

3. Add spinach and Bragg's, cover and cook 5 minutes or until tender.


# Apple Stuffed Acorn Squash

*Serves 4*

2 acorn **squash**
2 tart cooking **apples**
1 ½ tsp. grated **lemon rind**
1 T. fresh **lemon juice**
¼ cup melted **butter,** divided
⅓ cup pure **maple syrup**
**cinnamon**

1. Trim bottom point off each squash so the halves will be level when squash is served.

2. Cut each squash in half and scoop out seeds. Place in baking dish, cut side down, add ½ inch boiling water. Bake in 400° oven for 20 min.

3. Pare, core and dice apples. Place in a small bowl and mix with lemon rind, lemon juice 2 T. butter and maple syrup.

4. Brush squash halves with remaining 2 T. butter and sprinkle liberally with cinnamon.

5.  Fill squash halves with apple mixture. Place squash in baking dish. Add ½ inch boiling water, cover and bake 30 minutes. Before serving, pour pan juices over squash.

## Fennel Salad

*Serves 4*
*Different and delicious.*

2 **fennel bulbs**
4 **oranges,** peeled and sliced
¼ cup extra-virgin **olive oil**
2 T. **lemon juice**
1 tsp. **sea salt**
½ tsp. **pepper**
**arugula**

1.  Remove fennel fronds and chop a few to put on top of salad.
2.  Slice fennels in food processor, using slicing disc.
3.  Mix olive oil, lemon juice, salt and pepper in a small bowl.
4.  Put arugula in bottom of salad bowl, add fennel and orange slices.
5.  Drizzle dressing over top.

## Zucchini and Parsley Fritata

*Serves 2-3*

*Can also be baked in a 375° oven 20 min. or until puffed and browned.*

2 T. **butter**
1 T. extra-virgin **olive oil**
1 small **onion,** finely chopped
½ lb. **zucchini,** trimmed and chopped
½ lb. **tomatoes,** peeled, seeded and chopped
3 T. finely chopped **flat-leaf parsley**
**Herbamare** *and* **black pepper** to taste
4 large **eggs**

1.  Heat butter and oil in skillet. Add onion and saute until golden and tender.

2. Add zucchini, tomatoes, parsley, Herbamare and pepper.

3. Cook over low heat until zucchini is tender, about 8 min.

4. Break eggs into bowl and beat lightly. Season with a little more salt and pepper.

5. Pour over the zucchini mixture, stirring with a wooden spoon.

6. Turn the heat on very low and cook until the eggs have set.

7. Run the pan under the broiler to brown the top, if desired. Slide frittata out of pan and serve hot.

## Kale Chips

1 bunch **kale**
extra-virgin **olive oil**
**garlic powder**
**chipotle powder** *or* **smoked paprika**
**sea salt** to taste

1. Wash and dry kale thoroughly. Remove tough stems and rough chop.

2. Spread kale on cookie sheet lined with unbleached parchment paper.

3. Drizzle olive oil over kale, and toss with spices.

4. Bake at 350* 15 min. Salt to taste

## Easy Curried Eggplant

1 medium **eggplant,** unpeeled
3 T. extra-virgin **olive oil**
1 medium **onion,** chopped
1 T. fresh **gingerroot,** peeled and minced
5 cloves **garlic,** minced
2 tsp. ground **coriander**
2 tsp. ground **cumin**
½ tsp. **turmeric**
⅛ tsp. **cayenne**
2 T. **cilantro** *or* **parsley,** chopped

*Serves 4*

*Even people who think they don't like eggplant love this recipe.*

*Don't forget, both eggplant and curry are highly anti-cancer and anti-fungal.*

1 tsp. Herbamare
½ tsp. garlic powder
1 (28 oz.) can diced tomatoes.

---

1.  Slice eggplant and sprinkle with salt. Let stand for 1 hour, rinse and pat dry with paper towel. Cut into ¾ inch dice.

2.  Heat oil in heavy, wide casserole. Add onions and gingerroot and cook over low heat 7 min.

3.  Add garlic, coriander, cumin, turmeric, cayenne and 1 T. cilantro. Cook, stirring 1 minute.

4.  Add eggplant, Herbamare, and garlic powder and saute, stirring until eggplant is coated with spices.

5.  Add tomatoes and bring to a boil. Cover and simmer on low heat, stirring often, about 30 min. or until eggplant is very tender and mixture is thick. Adjust seasonings. Serve hot or cold, sprinkled with remaining 1 T. cilantro.

## Garden Vegetable Tabbouleh Salad

---

*Serves 8*

*Great alone, or as an accompaniment for chicken, lamb or fajitas.*

⅔ cup cracked **bulgur wheat**
2 medium **tomatoes**, finely chopped
¾ cup **parsley**, washed and finely minced
1 small carrot, finely chopped and parboiled
1 branch **broccoli**, peeled, finely chopped and parboiled
4 T. fresh **lemon juice**
2 T. extra-virgin **olive oil**
1 ½ tsp. **Herbamare**
1 T. **dried mint**

---

1.  Place bulgur in a bowl and pour in enough water to cover. Soak 30 min., drain and squeeze out excess water.

2. Place bulgur in a large salad bowl, add parsley, onion, carrot, and broccoli.

3. Combine lemon juice, oil, salt and mint and pour over bulgur. Chill thoroughly.

## Spicy Corn Stir Fry

---

1 **red bell pepper,** chopped
1 T. minced **jalapeno pepper**
2 T. **butter**
1 ½ tsp. ground **cumin**
2 cups **fresh corn,** *or* 1 (16 oz.) pkg. **frozen white shoepeg corn**
**Herbamare** to taste

---

*Serves 4*

1. Stir-fry pepper and jalapeno in butter over medium heat for 5 min.

2. Add cumin and stir-fry 30 sec.

3. Add corn and stir-fry 2 min. or until heated through.

## Artichoke and Tomatoes

---

4 T. **butter**
1 cup sliced **onions**
2 (16 oz.) cans **tomatoes,** drained
1 (14 oz.) can **artichoke hearts**
1 T. **dried basil**
**Herbamare** *and* **black pepper** to taste

---

*Serves 4*

*Eat artichokes frequently – they are highly anti-cancer and anti-fungal.*

1. Saute onions in butter until limp.

2. Add tomatoes, artichoke hearts and seasonings.

3. Heat through.

# Spaghetti Squash with Moroccan Spices

*Serves 4*

1 (2 lb.) **spaghetti squash**
1 large clove **garlic**, minced
2 T. **butter**
½ tsp. ground **cumin**
¼ tsp. ground **coriander**
dash **cayenne pepper**
½ tsp. **Herbamare**
2 T. chopped **fresh cilantro**

1. Cut spaghetti squash in half lengthwise. Scoop out seeds and discard.
2. Place cut side down in baking dish with small amount of water. Bake at 350° for 45 min. or until done. Skin should be tender. Cool 5 min.
3. While squash is cooling, cook garlic in butter in small saucepan, stirring, until golden, about 1 min. Stir in salt and spices and remove from heat.
4. Carefully scrape squash flesh with a fork, loosening and separating strands. Toss with flavored butter and cilantro.

# Broccoli Quiche

*Serves 4-6*

*Carrots and zucchini can be substituted for broccoli.*

I (9" or I0") homemade **pie crust** (p. 168)
1 cup chopped **broccoli**
1 cup chopped **onion**
1 cup grated yeast-free **almond** *or* **rice cheese**—
**Jack, cheddar,** *or* **mozzarella**
3 **eggs**
1 ½ cup **almond milk**
½ tsp. **Herbamare**
½ tsp. ground **nutmeg**

1. Pre-heat oven to 400° and bake crust 10 min. Remove from oven and reduce heat to 350°.

2. Steam broccoli and onions 2 min.

3. Place in crust the broccoli, onions and cheese.

4. In medium bowl, beat eggs lightly,add milk, Herbamare and nutmeg. Mix well and pour over vegetables and cheese.

5. Bake until set - around 40 min. Let stand 5 min. before slicing.

## Lemon-Buttered New Potatoes

2 lbs. small **new potatoes,** unpeeled and quartered
¼ cup **butter**
2 T. chopped **fresh parsley**
2 T. **lemon juice**
1 tsp. grated **lemon rind**
½ tsp. **Herbamare**
¼ tsp. **black pepper**
¼ tsp. ground **nutmeg**
**fresh parsley sprigs** for garnish

*Serves 8*

1. Cook potatoes in boiling water to cover until tender, about 10 min. Drain carefully, leaving skins intact.

2. Combine butter, parsley, lemon juice, lemon rind, Herbamare, pepper and nutmeg in a small saucepan. Cook over medium heat, stirring until butter melts.

3. Pour butter mixture over potatoes, tossing lightly to coat.

4. Garnish, if desired. Serve immediately.

## Spicy Sweet Potatoes

4 large **sweet potatoes** *or* **yams,** sliced 1 inch thick, with skin on
1 - 2 T. extra virgin **olive oil**

*Serves 4*

2 tsp. **garam masala**
2 tsp. ground **cumin**
**Herbamare** *and* **black pepper** to taste

_____

1. Put sliced potatoes on lightly oiled unbleached parchment paper on baking sheet. Brush with oil.
2. Sprinkle with remaining ingredients.
3. Bake at 375° 30 - 40 min. or until done.

## Garlic Mashed Potatoes

_____

4 boiling **potatoes**
4 large cloves **garlic,** peeled
½ stick **butter**
⅓ cup **almond milk**
1 tsp. **Herbamare**
½ tsp. **black pepper**

_____

*Serves 4*

*Grated fresh horseradish can be substituted for garlic. It's fabulous. Use at least 2 T. You can add the fresh garlic after cooking potatoes for more garlic punch.*

1. Cook potatoes and garlic in water to cover until done. Drain.
2. Add butter, milk, Herbamare and pepper, and cream in mixer or with potato masher. Serve immediately.

## Red Potato Salad with Watercress Mayonnaise

_____

2 lb. **red potatoes**
½ **red bell pepper,** chopped
½ cup **green onions,** chopped
1 cup **watercress mayonnaise** (p. 143)

_____

*Serves 4*

1. Cook potatoes in boiling salted water to cover until tender. Drain and cool. Cut into chunks.
2. Combine potatoes, red pepper, green onions and watercress

mayonnaise in a large bowl. Chill if you like.

3. Place on a bed of watercress and arrange tomato wedges around salad.

## Baked Potato with Veggie Sauce

4 baking potatoes
2 T. extra-virgin **olive oil**
½ cup each: **squash, zucchini, cauliflower,** *and* **carrots**
¼ cup **onions,** chopped
**Herbamare** to taste
**garlic powder** to taste
**black pepper** to taste
1 recipe for **Almond Cheese Sauce,** (p. 150)

*Serves 4*

*Rice or pasta can be
substituted for potatoes
for a change.*

1. Bake potatoes in 425° oven until done.

2. Saute in olive oil the squash, zucchini, cauliflower, carrots and
onions until tender. Season with Herbamare, garlic powder, and
pepper to taste.

3. Prepare Cheese Sauce (p.150).

4. Slice potatoes almost in two, spoon sauteed vegetables onto the
potatoes, and spread Almond Cheese Sauce over all.

## Baked Grits

1 scant cup **white** *or* **yellow grits,** not instant
2 cups **water**
2 cups **almond milk**
1 stick **butter**
1 tsp. **sea salt**

*Serves 4*

*This is so versatile you
can cook it at 300°- 400°
- just shorten or lengthen
cooking time. It should be
lightly browned on top.*

*Add 1 cup grated almond
or rice cheese, or pecorino
romano for a change.*

1. Bring water and almond milk to the boiling point.

2. Add grits and cook over medium heat until it starts boiling and
thickening, stirring constantly.

3. Remove from heat and add butter and salt.

4. Pour into greased baking dish and bake at 350° 1 hr.

## Lemon Lentils

*Serves 4*

--------------------

1 large **yellow onion,** chopped
3 cloves **garlic,** chopped
2 T. extra-virgin **olive oil**
1 ½ tsp. **cumin**
5 cups **water** *or* **chicken broth**
1 ½ cups **red lentils**
1 ½ tsp. **Herbamare**
1 **bay leaf**
rinds of two **lemons,** peeled

--------------------

1. Saute onions and garlic in oil 5 - 10 min, or until slightly browned.

2. Add cumin, water, rinsed lentils, Herbamare, and lemon peelings.
Cover and cook 20 - 25 min.

3. Remove bay leaf before serving.

## Curried Lentils

*Serves 4*

--------------------

1 cup **lentils**
3 cups **water** *or* **chicken broth**
2 large **onions,** chopped
1 tsp. **Herbamare**
3 T. **butter**
3 cloves **garlic,** minced
1 tsp. **curry powder**

--------------------

1. Combine lentils and water. Add one of the onions and Herbamare,
bring to a boil. Reduce heat and simmer, covered, 30 min. Drain.

2.	In a skillet, heat the butter, add remaining onion and garlic, and cook until they begin to brown. Add to lentils.

3.	Add curry powder, and cook until lentils are very tender, about 10 min. longer. Add more Herbamare if needed.

## Spicy Lentils

1 T. **butter**
1 **onion,** chopped
2 **garlic** cloves, minced
1 cup **lentils**
4 cups **water**
¼ tsp. **cinnamon**
½ tsp. **ginger**
½ tsp. **cloves**
⅛ tsp. **cayenne**
3 tsp. **cumin**
2 tsp. **Herbamare**
freshly ground **black pepper** to taste

*Serves 4*

*Turn this into a soup by adding more water or chicken broth.*

1.	Saute onion and garlic in butter until they begin to brown.

2.	Add lentils, water, cinnamon, ginger, cloves, cayenne, cumin, Herbamare and black pepper. Cook on low heat, covered, for 1 ½ hrs.

## Mexican Black Bean Salad

2 cans **black beans,** drained, about 30 ounces
1 (15 ounce) can **corn,** drained
2 **Roma tomatoes,** diced
⅓ cup diced **red bell pepper**
⅓ cup diced **red onion**
⅓ cup diced **green onions**

*Serves 6-8*

½ cup diced **fresh pineapple**
½ cup diced **cilantro**
1 **jalapeno pepper**, seeded and minced (opt.)
4 T. **lemon juice**
juice of half a **lime**
3 T. **honey**
1 T. **sea salt**
1 tsp. **black pepper**
1 tsp. **cumin**
**Herbamare** to taste

1. Mix all in a bowl and refrigerate at least one hour.

## Pureed Beans

*Serves 4*

*Wonderful with lamb, chicken and fish.*

2 (17oz.) cans **cannellini beans**, drained
¼ cup each extra-virgin **olive oil** *and* **butter**
3 T. chopped fresh **sage**, or 1 T. dried
1 tsp. **dried parsley**
½ tsp. **Herbamare**
freshly ground **black pepper** to taste
**Santay garlic powder** to taste

1. Heat butter and oil in skillet over moderate heat.
2. Add beans, sage, parsley, salt and pepper and cook 10 min.
3. Puree in food mill or food processor if you like.

## Green Beans Vinaigrette

*Serves 4*

2 lbs. **fresh green beans**
½ cup extra-virgin **olive oil**
2 tsp. lemon zest or **grated lemon rind**
¼ cup fresh **lemon juice**
2 cloves **garlic**, minced

1 tsp. **Herbamare**
¼ tsp. **crushed red pepper flakes**

———————————————————

1. Cook beans in small amount of water until tender—10 - 12 min.

2. Combine oil and rest of ingredients in a jar and shake vigorously.

3. Pour over beans in casserole dish and chill at least 2 hours. Turn occasionally.

## Sugar Snap Peas with Ginger and Garlic

———————————————————

¾ lb. **sugar snap peas,** trimmed
1 T. **olive oil**
1 T. finely chopped peeled **fresh ginger**
2 **shallots,** thinly sliced
1 **garlic** clove, finely chopped
½ cup **water**
**Herbamare** *and* **pepper** to taste

*Serves 4*

———————————————————

1. Heat oil in large skillet over moderately high heat until hot but not smoking.

2. Saute shallots, ginger and garlic, stirring 1 min.

3. Add peas and saute, stirring, 2 min.

4. Add water and simmer, stirring occasionally, until peas are crisp-tender, about 2 min.

5. Drain and season with salt and pepper.

## Baked Sweet Potato Fries

———————————————————

4 **sweet potatoes**
Extra-virgin **olive oil**
**Herbamare** to taste

*Serves 4-6*

———————————————————

1. Peel sweet potatoes and slice into fries-like slivers.

2. Place on parchment paper on cookie sheet in one layer.

3. Drizzle with olive oil and sprinkle with Herbamare.

4. Bake at 450* 15 min., turn and cook 5 - 10 min. longer.

## Black Bean Salad

*Serves 4*

*I love this recipe—
especially in the summer.
So full of flavor.*

*

1 (16 oz.) can **black beans,** drained
1 cup cooked **corn kernels**
½ cup **celery,** chopped
½ cup **green onion,** chopped
½ cup **sweet red pepper,** chopped
½ cup **cilantro,** chopped
1 - 2 **serrano chilies,** seeded and minced
3 cloves **garlic,** minced
2 tsp. fresh **gingerroot,** peeled and minced
3 T. **toasted oriental sesame oil**
3 T. freshly squeezed **lime juice**
**Herbamare** to taste

1. Combine beans, corn, celery, onion, red pepper, cilantro, chilies, garlic and gingerroot in a large bowl.

2. Whisk oil with lime juice in a small bowl. Pour dressing over bean mixture and toss to combine. Season with Herbamare, and chill well.

## Black-Eyed Pea Salsa

*This is great as an hors
d'oeuvre served with
yeast-free crackers, or
as a side dish.*

1 (16 oz.) can **black-eyed peas,** drained
1 **tomato,** chopped
1 bunch **green onions,** sliced
3 T. fresh **lime juice**
1 T. extra-virgin **olive oil**
2 cloves **garlic,** minced

1 tsp. ground **cumin**
1 tsp. **Herbamare**
1 T. chopped **fresh cilantro**

1. Place peas in colander. Rinse with cold water and drain.

2. Combine tomatoes and next 7 ingredients in a medium bowl.

3. Stir in peas, cover and refrigerate at least 4 hrs. Serve with tortilla chips or yeast-free crackers.

## Orzo with Zucchini

½ cup **orzo** (small rice-shaped pasta)
4 - 5 medium **zucchini** (about 3 lbs.) trimmed and sliced
¼ cup extra-virgin **olive oil**
1 tsp. **dried oregano**
**Herbamare** to taste

*Serves 4-6*

*Make this for lunch when zucchini is abundant in the garden.*

1. Fill a large pot with water, bring to a boil and add orzo. Reduce heat and cook for 15 min., or until tender, stirring occasionally t prevent sticking.

2. While orzo cooks, in a large heavy pot, saute zucchini in oil until lightly browned, about 5 min.

3. Add drained orzo to zucchini. Season with Herbamare, pepper and oregano. Cover and cook few more minutes, stirring carefully to prevent sticking. Serve hot or cold.

## Fettuccine Primavera

3 T. extra-virgin **olive oil**
2 cloves **garlic,** minced
1 head **broccoli,** thinly cut

*Serves 4-6*

1 large **red pepper,** thinly sliced
1 small **red onion,** thinly sliced
1 cup frozen **baby peas,** thawed
½ cup **fresh basil,** cut into strips
½ cup **black olives,** sliced
8 oz. **fettuccine pasta**
3 cups yeast-free **spaghetti sauce**

1. In a skillet, saute broccoli and garlic in oil for 5 min.

2. Add red pepper strips and red onion. Cook 5 - 10 min.

3. Stir in peas and cook a few more minutes.

4. Add olives, basil and spaghetti sauce. Cook until mixture is hot.

5. Pour over cooked pasta. Add extra garlic powder and Herbamare, if needed.

## Pasta with Peanuts and Orange Peel

8 oz. **angel hair** *or* **other thin noodle**
½ cup **scallions,** thinly sliced
½ cup **cilantro,** chopped
¼ cup light **olive oil**
¼ cup fresh **lemon juice**
2 T. **Bragg's Liquid Aminos**
grated rind of 2 large oranges
2 tsp. **toasted oriental sesame oil**
1 tsp. **sea salt**
¼ tsp. **dried red pepper** flakes
½ cup chopped **cocktail peanuts**

*Serves 4*

*Salad can be made a day in advance, but do not add peanuts until just before serving.*

1. Cook noodles, and drain thoroughly.

2. In large bowl, combine noodles, scallions and cilantro. Toss.

3. In small bowl, combine oil, lemon juice, Bragg's, peel, sesame oil, salt and pepper flakes. Whisk to blend.

4. Pour dressing over salad and add peanuts last. Serve immediately.

## Pasta Salad with Tomato-Lime Salsa

4 small **serrano chilies**
8 oz. dried **shell pasta**
extra-virgin **olive oil**
8 - 10 ripe **plum tomatoes,** (medium size, about 2" long)
1 small **red onion,** chopped
2 large bunches **cilantro,** chopped
**juice of 2 limes**
**Herbamare** *and* **black pepper** to taste

*Serves 4*

1.  Wash chilies, split in half, remove center, core and chop.

2.  Cook pasta al dente. Drain and toss with a little olive oil. Cool to room temperature.

3.  Coarsely chop tomatoes, combine with onion, chilies, cilantro, lime juice, Herbamare and pepper.

4.  Add salsa to pasta and toss lightly.


## Pasta with Pine Nuts

1 lb. **pasta** (vermicelli, spaghettini or angel hair)
1 T. extra-virgin **olive oil**
3 T. **garlic,** chopped
3 cups **tomatoes,** chopped
¾ cup **sun-dried tomatoes,** thinly sliced
½ cup **fresh basil,** chopped
½ cup **pine nuts**
1 cup **chicken stock**
**sea salt** *and* **black pepper** to taste

*Serves 4*

1.  Cook pasta until al dente.

2.  In a large skillet, heat oil and saute garlic until translucent.

3.  Add tomatoes, basil and pine nuts. Cook 2 - 3 min.

4.  Add chicken stock, salt and pepper. Toss with pasta. .

# Angel Hair with Garlic and Lemon

*Serves 4 as a main dish,
6-8 as a side.*

*Add pine nuts if you
want more protein.*

1 lb. **angel hair, spaghetti** *or* **capellini pasta**
4 large **garlic** cloves, minced
½ to ¾ tsp. **dried red pepper flakes**
½ cup extra-virgin **olive oil**
Finely grated **zest from 2 lemons**
3 T. fresh **lemon juice**
1 ½ tsp. **sea salt**
½ tsp. **black pepper**
½ cup chopped **cilantro** *or* **parsley**

1. Cook pasta in a 6 quart pot of salted water until al dente. Reserve 1 cup cooking water and drain pasta in colander.

2. Cook garlic and red pepper flakes in oil in a 12 inch skillet over moderate heat, stirring, until garlic is golden, about 5 minutes.

3. Stir in zest, then juice, salt, pepper and ½ cup reserved cooking water and bring to a simmer.

4. Toss pasta in sauce with cilantro. Add cooking water if pasta is dry.

# Quick Black Beans and Rice

*Serves 4*

*Guacamole is perfect
with this.*

1 (16 oz.) can **black beans**
1 medium **onion,** chopped
1 **tomato,** chopped
½ tsp. **Herbamare**
½ tsp. **cumin**
½ tsp. **chili powder**
chopped **fresh cilantro**
1 cup **basmati rice,** cooked

1. Heat beans, liquid included, with onion, tomato, Herbamare, cumin, and chili powder for 10 min.

2. Serve with cooked rice and sprinkle chopped cilantro on top.

## Wild Rice Salad

---

1 cup **wild rice**
¼ cup fresh **lemon juice**
¼ cup extra-virgin **olive oil**
¼ cup **Bragg's Liquid Aminos**
3 T. minced fresh **garlic**
3 T. minced, peeled, fresh **gingerroot**
3 cups **mung** or **sunflower sprouts** (½ pound)
1 cup chopped, trimmed **snow peas** (¼ pound)

*Serves 4-6*

*Use sprouts sparingly and wash well as they tend to have high mold counts.*

---

1. In a saucepan add enough water to cover rice by several inches and bring to a boil. Reduce heat and simmer 30 - 40 min. until tender. Drain and rinse.

2. In a medium bowl, whisk together lemon juice, oil, Bragg's, garlic, ginger root.

3. Add rice, sprouts and snow peas, tossing well to combine.

## Almond Rice Pilaf

---

⅔ cup **almonds,** sliced
3 T. **butter,** divided
1 cup **onion,** chopped
2 cloves **garlic,** finely chopped
1 small **green bell pepper,** chopped
1 cup **basmati** or other **long-grain white rice**
1 tsp. **cumin**
½ tsp. **sea salt**
1 ¾ cup **chicken broth**

*Serves 4-6*

---

1. Saute almonds in 1 T. butter until golden. Reserve.

2. Saute onion and garlic in remaining 2 T. butter until translucent.

3. Add green pepper, rice, cumin, chicken broth and salt. Bring to a boil, reduce heat to low, and cook covered 20 min. or until all liquid

is absorbed. Remove from heat and let stand covered 5 min.

4. Stir in almonds and serve.

## Baked Brown and Wild Rice

Serves 4

One of the most delicious
of my rice recipes.

1 cup **brown rice/wild rice mix**
1 cup **chicken** *or* **beef broth** (yeast free—for beef broth use ⅛ cup
Bragg's Liquid Aminos to ¾ cup water)
½ cup **water**
½ cup **butter**
½ can **water chestnuts**, sliced
2 stalks **celery**, chopped
½ cup chopped **onions**

1. Mix all together in a casserole. Cover and bake at 350° 1 hour or until all the liquid is absorbed. Stir a couple of times.

## Lemon Rice Pilaf

Serves 6

Also delicious with just
the rind and juice, added
after the rice is cooked.

2 T. **butter**
4 stalks **celery**, sliced
6 **green onions**, chopped
3 cups hot **cooked rice**
2 T. grated **lemon rind**
**juice of one lemon**
**Herbamare** *and* **pepper** to taste.

1. Melt butter in a large skillet over medium-high heat. Add celery and green onions and saute until tender. Stir in cooked rice and remaining ingredients.

2. Cook until thoroughly heated.

## Carrot and Turnip Puree

2 lbs. **carrots,** peeled and cut into 2 inch lengths
2 large **turnips,** (8 oz.) peeled and quartered
¼ cup **parsley,** firmly packed, and finely minced
3 T. **butter**
1 tsp. **nutmeg,** freshly grated
1 tsp. **Herbamare**
½ tsp. freshly ground **black pepper**

*Serves 6-8*

*This is a must during the holidays, but I get requests for it all during the year.*

1. Cover carrots with water and cook until tender. Cook turnips in salted water, covered, until tender. Drain both.

2. Put carrots and turnips in food processor and mix until pureed, about 10 sec.

3. Place in bowl, add butter and seasonings.

4. Bake 30 - 40 min. in 350° oven. Sprinkle with chopped parsley.

## Turnip Pudding

8 fresh **turnips,** peeled and sliced (about 2 ½ lbs.)
**water** to cover
½ tsp. **sea salt**
½ cup **onion,** chopped
2 T. **butter**
¼ cup **almond milk**
2 large **eggs,** lightly beaten
½ tsp. **Herbamare**
¼ tsp. **black pepper**
½ tsp. ground **nutmeg**

*Serves 6*

1. Combine turnips, salt, and water in a saucepan. Bring to a boil, cover and cook over medium heat until turnips are tender, 10 - 15 min.

2. Drain turnips and mash well with potato masher or mix in electric mixer.

3. Cook onion in butter over medium heat, stirring constantly until tender. Remove from heat, stir in turnips, milk, and remaining ingredients.

4. Spoon into a greased 8" baking dish and bake at 350° 35 - 40 min. or until set. Serve immediately.

# Quinoa Salad

---

3 T. **lemon juice**
3 T. **olive oil**
3 T. **cilantro,** minced
1 cup **fresh** *or* **frozen corn**
½ cup **quinoa,** thoroughly rinsed
1 - 2 tsp. **cumin**
1 cup cooked or canned **black beans**
3 T. **red onion,** minced
**salt** *and* **pepper** to taste

---

*Serves 3-4*

*If using leftover quinoa, I skip cooking the corn. Just add frozen—works fine.*

1. Combine lemon juice, olive oil, cilantro, salt and pepper and set aside.

2. Bring 1 ½ cups water to a boil in a small saucepan and add corn. Reduce heat and simmer until corn is tender. Drain corn, reserving 1 cup of the cooking liquid.

3. Return cooking liquid to the saucepan and bring to a boil. Add quinoa and cumin. Cover and simmer 10 min. until all liquid is absorbed.

4. Remove quinoa from heat and set aside 5 min.

5. Fluff quinoa with fork and transfer to a salad bowl. Cool slightly.

6. Add corn, black beans and onion to quinoa.

7. Add dressing and chill.

## Quinoa Rutabaga Patties

1 cup **quinoa,** cooked
1 cup **rutabaga,** grated
¼ cup **shallots,** finely diced
1 large clove **garlic,** minced
¼ cup fresh **chives,** finely minced
¼ cup **parsley,** finely minced
2 **eggs,** lightly beaten
½ tsp. **turmeric**
½ tsp. **sea salt**
¼ tsp. freshly ground **black pepper**
2 T. **olive oil** *or* **coconut oil**

*Serves 4*
*These are fun to make and the kiddies love them as well.*

1. Preheat oven to 400°.

2. In a large bowl add quinoa, rutabaga, shallots, parsley, chives,, garlic, eggs turmeric, salt and pepper and combine thoroughly.

3. Put unbleached parchment paper on rimmed baking sheet and brush with olive oil.

4. Using a ¼ cup measuring cup, scoops mounds of patty mixture onto baking sheet and flatten with back of fork to a thickness of 1 inch.

5. Bake patties for 10 minutes, then flip and bake for another 10 minutes.


## Roasted Cauliflower with Garlic

1 whole head of **garlic,** cloves separated but not peeled
1 large head of **cauliflower,** trimmed and cut into large florets
5 T. extra-virgin **olive oil,** divided
2 tsp. **sea salt** and 1 tsp. freshly ground **black pepper**
½ cup minced fresh **parsley**
3 - 4 T. **pine nuts,** toasted in a small pan until lightly browned
2 T. freshly squeezed **lemon juice**

*Serves 4-6*

*This is my favorite recipe for cauliflower. The flavor is wonderful and cauliflower is one of the best anti-fungal veggies you can eat.*

1. Bring a small pan of water to the boil, and add garlic cloves. Boil for exactly 15 seconds, then drain and peel. Cut any large cloves in half.

2. In a glass casserole, toss the cauliflower with the garlic, 3 T. of the olive oil, 2 tsp. sea salt and 1 tsp. pepper.

3. Spread the mixture into a single layer and roast 20 - 25 minutes at 450*, stirring twice.

4. Pour the mixture into a large bowl, add the remaining 2 T. olive oil, the parsley, pine nuts and lemon juice.

5. Sprinkle with another ½ tsp. sea salt, toss, and serve hot or warm.

## Sesame Kale Salad

1 large clove **garlic,** finely minced
2 1/2 tsp. **toasted sesame oil**
1 1/2 T. extra-virgin **olive oil**
3 T. **lemon juice**
2 T. **Bragg's Liquid Aminos**
10 cups packed, chopped **kale** leaves, thick stems removed
**sea salt** and **black pepper**

1. In a large bowl whisk together the garlic, sesame oil, olive oil, lemon juice and Bragg's Liquid Aminos

2. Add the kale and massage it with your hands (very important!) untilit has become shiny and reduced in volume by one third to one half.

3. Season with sea salt and pepper and toss well.

4. Refrigerate.

# Pestos, Dressings, Sauces, and Dips

*"Command the Israelites to bring you clear oil of pressed olives for the light so that the lamps may be kept burning "*

—EXODUS 27:20

Pestos are fun and easy to make as well as nutritious. Use them liberally on pastas, sandwiches, baked potatoes, in soups, spread over fish, or use as a dip.

The quickest and easiest way to dress a salad in my house is to simply drizzle extra-virgin olive or macadamia nut oil over the salad, add lemon or lime juice, sprinkle on Herbamare and toss. Also good on slaws of all kinds. Here are a few of the other dressings we like.

*Basil Pesto*

## Cilantro Pesto

---

¼ cup **pine nuts** *or* **pecans**
2 cloves **garlic**
¼ tsp. **sea salt**
1 cup firmly packed **cilantro leaves**
3 T. extra-virgin **olive oil**
2 T. yeast-free **rice** *or* **almond parmesan cheese**

---

1. In a small skillet, toast pine nuts and whole garlic cloves until lightly brown, stirring so nuts don't burn.
2. Put all in food processor and blend well. Cover and refrigerate.

## Basil Pesto

---

2 cups fresh **basil leaves**
¼ cup **pine nuts,** lightly toasted
2 - 4 cloves **garlic,** to taste
½ tsp. **sea salt**
1 T. fresh **lemon juice**
2 T. extra virgin **olive oil**
¼ cup yeast-free **rice** *or* **almond parmesan cheese**

---

1. Place all ingredients in food processor and blend until smooth. Cover and refrigerate.

## Arugula Pesto

---

2 cloves **garlic**
½ cup **chopped pecans,** toasted 10 min. in 350° oven
3 cups packed **arugula leaves**
3 T. yeast-free **rice** *or* **almond parmesan cheese**
1 T. **lemon juice**

½ tsp. **Herbamare** *and* freshly ground **pepper**

⅓ cup extra-virgin **olive oil**

---

## Basic French Dressing

---

½ cup extra-virgin **olive oil** *or* **nut oil**

¼ cup fresh **lemon juice**

1 clove **garlic,** crushed

½ tsp. **dried tarragon**

½ tsp. **dried thyme**

½ tsp. **Herbamare**

---

1. Mix well and refrigerate until ready to use.

## Cucumber Dressing

---

½ cup **homemade mayonnaise,** (p. 142)

1 cup **cucumber,** peeled and diced

1 tsp. **dried tarragon**

1 tsp. **dried dill weed**

½ tsp. **dry mustard**

2 tsp. fresh **lemon juice**

½ tsp. **Herbamare**

---

1. Blend all in a blender or food processor on low speed.

## Sesame Dressing 1

---

1 T. fresh **garlic,** minced

1 T. **fresh ginger,** peeled and minced

*Good on pastas, veggies, salad, rice, anything and everything!*

5 - 6 T. **Bragg's Liquid Aminos**
1 T. fresh **lemon juice**
1 T. toasted **sesame oil**
¾ tsp. **hot red pepper flakes** (opt.)
2 T. **homemade mayonnaise,** (p. 142)
¼ cup extra-light **olive oil**

_____

1.	Mix together with a whisk, cover and refrigerate.

## Creamy Vinaigrette
_____

¼ cup fresh **lemon juice**
2 T. **homemade mayonnaise** (p. 142)
1 large clove **garlic,** minced
⅔ cup extra-virgin **olive oil**
**sea salt** *and* **black pepper** to taste

_____

1.	Measure lemon juice and mayonnaise into a 2 cup measuring cup.

2.	With a small whisk stir in garlic, a big pinch of salt and a few grinds of pepper.

3.	Slowly whisk olive oil into the mixture, first in droplets, then in a slow steady stream to make an emulsified vinaigrette. Cover and refrigerate.

## Tahini Dressing
_____

*Exotic and very tasty.*

⅔ cup **tahini** (ground sesame seeds)
⅓ cup **Bragg's Liquid Aminos**
2 T. fresh **lemon juice**
8 T. **water**

_____

1.	Stir together and refrigerate. Add more water if you like it thinner.

## Sesame Dressing 2

½ cup **homemade mayonnaise,** (p. 142)
1 T **toasted sesame oil**
1 T. **Bragg's Liquid Aminos**
1 tsp. **garlic powder**

1. Whisk together and refrigerate.

## Avocado Dressing

1 large ripe **avocado**
1 clove **garlic,** minced
1 T. fresh **lemon juice**
½ tsp. **Veg-Sal**
2 - 4 T. **homemade mayonnaise** (p. 142)

*Add chopped tomato, onion, or cilantro for a change.*

1. Blend on low speed in blender or food processor until smooth.

## Green Goddess Dressing

½ cup **homemade mayonnaise,** (p. 142)
1 tsp. **dried dill weed**
2 T. fresh **parsley,** finely chopped
1 T. **lemon juice**
1 T. extra-virgin **olive oil**
½ tsp. **Herbamare**

1. Mix ingredients, thinning with extra olive oil and lemon juice if you like a thinner dressing.
2. Pour over raw or cooked vegetables.

## Susan's Dressing

*I've made this with red and yellow peppers, also.*

1 **green pepper**
2 stalks **celery**
⅔ cup fresh **lemon juice**
⅔ cup **Bragg's Liquid Aminos**
1 cup **sesame tahini**
⅔ cup light **olive oil**

1. Put green pepper, celery, lemon juice, Bragg's, and tahini in food processor and chop well.
2. Slowly add oil until oil is incorporated.
3. Chill. Add a little water if too thick.

## Mayonnaise 1

*Easy and fun to make, homemade mayonnaise tastes so much better you may never buy "store-bought" again.*

*There are many recipes for mayonnaise. Here are two. One is a whole egg recipe, and the other calls for just the yolk. There are only two important tricks to remember when making mayonnaise. The first is to be Sure to remove all the tiny lemon seeds from the lemon juice since just one little seed can break down the emulsion. The other is to pour the oil slowly in a thin stream when being added. Both recipes are easily doubled, but don't do it until you get the hang of it.*

1 **egg**—room temperature
2 T. freshly squeezed **lemon juice**
1 tsp. **dry mustard**
½ tsp. **Herbamare**
few shakes **cayenne**
¾ cup light **olive oil**
¼ cup extra-virgin **olive oil**

1. Put egg, lemon juice, mustard, cayenne and Herbamare in blender or food processor.
2. Turn on high and slowly add oils while the machine is running. Blend until smooth. Refrigerate immediately.

## Mayonnaise 2

1 **egg yolk**—room temperature
½ tsp. **sea salt**

½ tsp. **dry mustard** *and* few shakes **cayenne**
2 T. freshly squeezed **lemon juice**
¾ cup **light olive** or **nut oil**

1. Put yolk, salt, mustard, cayenne, and lemon juice in blender or food processor.
2. Turn on high and slowly add oil while machine is running. Blend until smooth. Refrigerate immediately.

## Watercress Mayonnaise

1 cup **homemade mayonnaise** (above)
½ cup **watercress,** chopped
1 tsp. **dried dill weed**
1 tsp. fresh **lemon juice**
¼ tsp. **Herbamare**
⅛ tsp. **black pepper**

*Good on everything. I put it on sandwiches, wraps, veggies, potatoes, pastas, etc.*

1. Combine all in food processor or blender and blend until smooth. Refrigerate.

## Almondaise

½ cup raw **almonds** with skins
¾ cup **almond milk**
2 tsp. **almond flour**
¼ tsp. **garlic powder**
1 ½ cups light **olive oil**
1 tsp. **Herbamare**
3 T. fresh **lemon juice**

*(for those who are allergic to eggs)*

1. Place almonds in a food processor and grind into a fine powder.
2. Add almond milk, almond flour, garlic powder, and Herbamare.

Blend well to form a smooth cream.

3.  Turn processor on and add oil in a thin stream until mixture is thick.

4.  Add lemon juice and cover tightly.

## Homemade Ketchup

---

1 cup **tomato sauce** *or* **paste**
⅓ cup **lemon juice**
¼ tsp. **sea salt**
½ tsp. **dried oregano**
⅛ tsp. **cumin**
⅛ tsp. **nutmeg**
⅛ tsp. **black pepper**
¼ tsp. **dry mustard**
¼ tsp. **garlic powder**

---

*If you use tomato sauce, add 2T. tomato paste to thicken a little.*

*You can make a quickie ketchup with just tomato paste, lemon juice, Bragg's Liquid Aminos, and Herbamare.*

1.  Mix well in a small bowl or blender. Refrigerate.

## Homemade Mustard

---

3 T. unbleached **white** *or* **rice flour**
1 ½ T. **dry mustard**
⅛ tsp. **turmeric**
⅛ tsp. ground **cloves**
⅓ cup fresh **lemon juice**
½ cup **boiling water**

---

*Keeps 2-3 weeks.*

1.  In small saucepan mix together flour, mustard, turmeric, and cloves.

2.  With a wire whisk, whisk in boiling water.

3.  Cook until very thick on medium heat, whisking occasionally.

4.  Remove from heat and stir in lemon juice gradually, whisking until smooth. Refrigerate.

## Tartar Sauce

½ cup **homemade mayonnaise** (p. 142)
2 T. fresh or frozen **chives**
1 tsp. fresh **lemon juice**
1 tsp. **dried tarragon**
1 tsp. **dried dill weed**
**sea salt** *or* **Herbamare** to taste

1.  Mix well in small bowl. Refrigerate.

## Hollandaise Sauce

3 **egg yolks**
2 T. freshly squeezed **lemon juice**
1 stick **butter,** melted
2 T. **hot water**
¼ tsp. **sea salt**
few grains **cayenne**

*Truly the queen of sauces —good on asparagus, broccoli, green beans, artichokes, fish, chicken, etc.*

1.  In a small saucepan put three egg yolks and beat with a wire whisk until smooth but not fluffy.

2.  Add lemon juice, butter, hot water, salt and cayenne. Set over medium low heat and whisk until sauce thickens. Do not over-cook.

3.  Take off heat and serve immediately.

## Guacamole

3 ripe, medium **avocados,** peeled, seeded, and coarsely mashed
3 T. fresh **lemon juice**
2 medium **tomatoes,** seeded and chopped

A can of chopped green chilies can be added if you like it hotter.

You can spread on sandwiches instead of mayonnaise for a change.

¼ cup minced **onion** (red, yellow *or* green)
½ cup **cilantro**, chopped
2 cloves **garlic**, minced
1 tsp. **Herbamare**

_____

1. In a medium bowl, mash avocado with fork.

2. Add lemon juice, tomatoes, onion, cilantro, garlic and Herbamare.

3. Mix well and serve with corn or tortilla chips. Makes about 4 cups.

## Picco de Gallo

_____

2 cups **Roma tomatoes**, diced
½ cup **yellow onions**, diced
¼ cup **cilantro**, chopped
1 T. fresh **garlic**, minced
4 T. fresh **lemon juice**
2 T. fresh **lime juice**
1 small **jalapeno** *or* **serrano pepper,** seeded and chopped
1 tsp. **Herbamare**
½ tsp. **black pepper**

_____

1. Mix all in a small mixing bowl and refrigerate.

2. Use as a dip for tortilla chips, with bean soups, or add extra-virgin olive oil to make a salad.

## White Bean Hummus

_____

2 cloves **garlic**
1 T. fresh or 1 tsp. dried **rosemary**
2 (15 oz.) cans **great northern beans,** rinsed and drained
3 T. fresh **lemon juice**
3 T. **tahini**
¾ tsp. **Herbamare**

¼ tsp. **ground red pepper**—opt.
¼ cup extra-virgin **olive oil**
**paprika** for garnish

---

1. Pulse garlic and rosemary in a food processor 3 or 4 times until minced.

2. Add beans and next 4 ingredients, process until smooth.

3. Pour olive oil gradually through food chute with processor still running. Process until smooth.

4. Cover and chill. Garnish with paprika and serve with crackers and raw veggies.

## Black Bean Hummus

---

1 large clove **garlic**, peeled
2 T. fresh **lemon juice**
1 T. **sesame tahini**
1 tsp. ground **cumin**
1 (15 oz.) can **black beans**
1 small **jalapeno pepper**, chopped
1 pinch **crushed red pepper**
2 tsp. extra-virgin **olive oil**
**Herbamare** to taste

*Serve with chips, crackers, or veggies.*

---

1. Chop garlic in food processor. Add lemon juice, tahini, cumin, salt, black beans, pepper, and process until smooth.

2. Drizzle with a little extra olive oil.

## Mary's Hummus

---

1 (16 oz.) can **garbanzo beans**, drained
¼ cup **toasted sesame tahini**
3 T. extra-virgin **olive oil**

*Great as a dip for
crackers, chips and raw
veggies. Also makes a
wonderful sandwich on
tortilla bread, either plain
or with sprouts, tomatoes,
and cucumbers.*

¼ cup **yellow onion,** chopped
4 **garlic** cloves, minced
1 T. fresh **lemon juice**
½ tsp. **cumin**
¼ tsp. **cayenne**
1 tsp. **garlic salt**

1.  Put all ingredients in blender and blend until smooth. Refrigerate.

## Peanut Tofu Dip

1 (10.5 oz.) **tofu**
3 T. **honey**
4 T. **smooth peanut butter**

*This is wonderful with
fresh fruit in the morning
for breakfast. Sliced ap-
ples, pears and strawber-
ries are particularly good.*

1.  Blend well in blender or food processor

2.  Refrigerate immediately.

## Spinach Dip

1 (10 oz.) pkg. **frozen chopped spinach**
1 cup **homemade mayonnaise,** (p. 142)
1 cup soft **tofu**
1 cup **parsley,** chopped
1 ½ T. fresh **lemon juice**
1 T. **dried dill weed**
1 tsp. **Fine Herbs** (Spice Island)
1 tsp. **Herbamare**

*Serve with raw broccoli,
cauliflower, radishes,
peppers, zucchini.*

*This is also good as a
sandwich filling with
tortillas, and is excel-
lent on baked potatoes
and cooked vegetables.*

1.  Thaw and drain spinach. Wring dry in paper towels.

2.  Combine rest of ingredients and stir in spinach.

3.  Cover and refrigerate until chilled—24 hours is best.

# Eggplant Dip

2 medium **eggplants**
3 cloves **garlic**
¼ cup **tahini**
**juice of one lemon**
⅓ tsp. **cumin**
1 tsp. **Jane's Crazy Mixed-Up Salt**
½ tsp. **Herbamare**
½ - 1 tsp. **garlic salt**
¼ cup toasted **sesame seeds**

*For eggplant lovers only.*

1.  Preheat oven to 375°. Pierce eggplant to prevent exploding and place in shallow baking pan.

2.  Bake until soft and shriveled, about 45 min to 1 hour.

3.  Remove from oven and cool on plate.

4.  When cool, cut in half and scrape pulp from skins. Place pulp in blender with rest of ingredients and blend until smooth.

5.  Chill and stir in sesame seeds. Add more seasonings if necessary.

# Hearts of Palm Dip

1 large **garlic** clove
**sea salt**
2 (14 oz.) cans **hearts of palm,** drained
¼ cup extra-virgin **olive oil**
1 tsp. finely grated **lime zest**
1 tsp. **Herbamare**
freshly ground **pepper**

*One of my favorite dips. Low-cal, high nutrition and fabulous.*

*Serve with chips or crackers. Also good in mashed potatoes.*

1.  Using the side of a chef's knife, mash the garlic to a paste with a generous pinch of salt. Scrape the paste into a food processor.

2. Add the hearts of palm and the oil and process to a medium-
fine paste.

3. Add the lime zest, season with salt and pepper, and pulse just to blend.

## Sun-Dried Tomato Pesto

*Serve with yeast-free crackers.*

½ cup **walnuts**
1 (8 oz.) jar **sun-dried tomatoes** in oil
2 large cloves **garlic**
2 T. extra-virgin **olive oil**
2 T. **tomato paste**
½ cup **pecorino romano** *or* **parmesan-style cheese substitute**
½ tsp. **sea salt**
¼ tsp. **black pepper**

1 Lightly toast walnuts in toaster oven. Cool and chop lightly.

2 In food processor, pulse tomatoes with oil, garlic, walnuts, tomato
paste, olive oil, salt and pepper.

3 Stir in cheese.

## Cheese Sauce

*Almond cheddar styles
can be used also.*

*Leave off all cheeses if you
want a plain white sauce.*

2 T. **butter**
2 T. unbleached **white flour**
1 cup, **almond, coconut,** *or* **rice milk**
½ tsp. **sea salt**
¼ tsp. **black pepper**
½ cup **parmesan-style grated cheese substitute**
(or pecornio romano in third month)

1. Melt butter in small saucepan, add flour and cook 1 min.

2. Add milk, salt and pepper, and cook over medium heat stirring

constantly until thick.

3. Add cheese and stir until melted.

## Peanut Sauce

⅓ cup natural smooth **peanut butter**
1 tsp. **garlic powder**
2 T. **lemon juice**
2 T. **Bragg's Liquid Aminos**
⅓ cup **water**

*Pour over pastas, chicken or other dishes.*

1. Heat well.

*Cherry Ice Cream p. 171*

# Desserts

*"See how my eyes brightened when I tasted a little of this honey. "*

...I SAMUEL...14:29

In all desserts calling for pure maple syrup, I use the dark, grade B. It is much more flavorful than the lighter, amber colored syrups. Remember, honey and maple syrup are healing and good for you in moderate amounts. In the first month, restrict desserts to 2 - 3 servings a week.

This may seem like a lot of dessert recipes to be in a yeast-free cookbook, but I have heard from so many people saying they would like to continue cooking without refined sugars even after the diet is over. Since I am always searching for really good yeast-free desserts, I am sharing the best I have found to date.

## Tapioca Pudding

*Serves 4*
*Good warm or cold.*

½ cup granulated **tapioca**
1 ½ cups **almond milk**
1 ½ cups **water**
¼ tsp. **sea salt**
2 **eggs**
1 tsp. pure **vanilla extract**
¼ cup pure **maple syrup**

1. Combine tapioca, almond milk, water and salt and bring to a boil. Simmer 2 min. on low heat. Add maple syrup.

2. Beat eggs, then beat in some of the hot tapioca.

3. Return all to pan and cook 3 min. on low heat, stirring constantly.

4. Cool 15 min. and add vanilla.

## Maple Mocha Pudding

*Serves 5*

3 T. **cornstarch**
1 T. **Pero** (instant coffee substitute)
1 tsp. **unsweetened carob powder**
¼ tsp. **sea salt**
3 **egg yolks**
3 cups **almond milk**
½ cup pure **maple syrup**
1 T. **butter**
1 tsp. pure **vanilla extract**

1. Combine cornstarch, Pero, carob powder, and salt in a 2 qt. pan. Stir to mix.

2. In a mixing bowl, whisk the egg yolks slightly, then add milk and maple syrup.

3. Stir into first mixture and bring to a boil over medium-high heat, stirring constantly with whisk or spatula.

4. Let boil 1 min, stirring.

5. Remove from heat and stir in butter and vanilla.

6. Pour into 5 custard cups or dessert bowls. To prevent a skin from forming, place a piece of wax paper, cut to size, on top of each.

7. Cool, then refrigerate for several hours before serving.


## Baked Maple Custard

---

3 **eggs**
½ cup pure **maple syrup**
2 cups **almond milk**
¼ tsp. **sea salt**

---

*Serves 4*

*For carob custard, use 2 C. carob Rice Dream and add ½ tsp. almond extract.*

1. Very lightly mix together all ingredients and pour into four greased custard cups.

2. Place cups in pan with sides, and pour hot water in pan until water comes about halfway up the cups.

3. Bake at 350° about 25 - 35 min, or until the edges seem set but the middle is a bit wiggly; they'll finish cooking as they cool.

4. Good warm, room temperature, or cold.


## Saucy Apples and Pears

---

3 **cooking apples,** cored and sliced (1 ½ lbs.)
3 ripe **pears,** cored and sliced (1 ½ lbs.)
1 T. fresh **lemon juice**
¼ cup melted **butter**
2 (3 inch) sticks **cinnamon**
½ cup **maple syrup**
1 T. **cornstarch**
2 T. **water**

---

*Serves 4*

*Some crock pots cook a lot faster than others. This recipe cooks in 4 hours in mine.*

1. Place apples and pears in a crock pot and sprinkle with lemon juice, tossing to coat well.

2. Add butter, cinnamon and maple syrup. Cook on low until done—6 - 8 hours.

3. Mix cornstarch and water and add last 15 min.

## Avocado Carob Cookies

4 oz. **unsweetened carob chips,** melted with
1 T. organic **coconut oil**
1 **avocado**
4 T. **almond butter**
⅔ cup **honey**
2 **eggs** *and* 2 **egg whites**
4 T. **carob powder**
3 T. **almond flour**
1 tsp. **sea salt**

*This is a surprising recipe.*
*Surprisingly good!*

1. In food processor puree avocado until smooth.

2. Add rest of ingredients one at a time and pulse until combined. Keep batter in refrigerator for one hour.

3. Put parchment paper on cookie sheet and place cookies on the paper using a smallish spoon.

4. Bake at 350* for 15 - 17 minutes.

5. Cool on rack.

## Baked Stuffed Pears

4 medium-sized ripe **pears**
2 T. fresh **lemon juice**
⅓ cup coarsely chopped **walnuts** *or* **pecans**
¼ cup chopped **apple**

*Serves 4*
*Serve warm or cold.*

1 tsp. finely grated **lemon zest**
½ tsp. **cinnamon**
3 T. pure **maple syrup**
⅔ cup **apple juice**
1 T. **butter,** quartered

---

1. Preheat oven to 350°. Core pears and cut a thin slice off bottom of each so pears will stand upright.

2. Place pears into baking dish and drizzle lemon juice over tops.

3. Combine nuts, apples, lemon zest, cinnamon and maple syrup in a small bowl. Stuff pear cavities with the filling and dot each with butter.

4. Pour apple juice into bottom of baking dish and bake for 1 hr. basting frequently.

## Oatmeal Coconut Bars

*Crust:*

1 1/2 cups uncooked **oatmeal**
2 T. melted **butter** or **coconut oil**
1/4 cup pure **maple syrup**

*Topping:*

1 cup **unsweetened carob chips**
1/2 cup chopped **walnuts** or **pecans**
1 cup shredded **unsweetened coconut**
1/4 cup pure **maple syrup**
1 tsp. **vanilla**
1 **egg,** beaten

---

1. Mix crust ingredients thoroughly.

2. Press mixture evenly over the bottom of a lightly oiled 8-inch square baking pan.

3. Stir together topping ingredients.

4. Spread mixture evenly over oatmeal crust.

5. Bake for 25 minutes at 350* until golden brown and cut into bars..

## Simple Fruit Cobbler

*Serves 6-8*

*Always a hit.*

½ cup **all-purpose flour**
½ cup **rolled oats**
½ cup **butter**
1 tsp. **baking powder**
½ tsp. ground **cinnamon**
2 T. slivered **almonds**
1 large **egg**
5 cups **combined fresh fruit,** such as blackberries, apples, blueberries, pears, peaches, cranberries, roughly diced
⅔ cup **maple syrup**
1 - 2 T. **cornstarch** *or* **arrowroot**

1. Place flour, oats, butter, baking powder and cinnamon in a food processor. Pulse quickly until blended.

2. Add almonds and pulse until chopped. Add egg and pulse four times or until mixture resembles coarse meal.

3. Toss fruit in a bowl with syrup and cornstarch. Lightly oil a 9 inch baking dish and spread fruit mixture on bottom. Crumble oat mixture on top.

4. Bake at 350° 35 min. or until bubbly. Top with Tofu Cream, if you like, recipe below.

## Basic Tofu Cream

*Serves 4-6*

1 (12.3 oz.) **Mori-Nu Silken Tofu** (firm)
2 T. extra light **olive oil**
½ tsp. **sea salt**

2 T. fresh **lemon juice**

1 T. **vanilla extract**

2 T. pure **maple syrup**

---

1.  Blend all in food processor or blender, cover and chill.

## Coconut Macaroons

1 ¼ cup **unsweetened coconut** (found in health food stores)

1 ¼ cup unbleached **white flour**

1 T. Rumford **baking powder**

¾ cup pure **maple syrup** *or* **honey**

¼ cup **water**

¼ cup light **olive oil**

1 **egg white,** beaten

1 tsp. pure **almond extract**

*Makes 24*

*For carob macaroons,*
*substitute ¼ cup carob for*
*¼ cup flour.*

1.  In a large mixing bowl, combine the coconut, flours and baking powder.

2.  In a separate bowl, whisk together the maple syrup, water, oil, beaten egg white and almond extract. Stir into dry mixture just until blended.

3.  Spoon rounded tablespoons of dough onto greased baking sheet, leaving 2" between cookies. Bake at 350° 12 - 15 min. Should be slightly soft. Cool on rack.

## Pumpkin Butter

1 (15oz.) can **pumpkin**

½ cup **apple juice**

½ cup **honey**

½ tsp. **cinnamon** *and* **nutmeg**
¼ tsp. **cloves**

1. Bring all ingredients to a boil, lower heat and simmer 15 min. until dark and thick

# Pumpkin Cookies

½ cup **butter**
1 cup pure **maple syrup**
1 cup canned **pumpkin**
1 **egg**
1 cup **whole wheat flour**
1 cup **unbleached white flour**
1 tsp. Rumford **baking powder**
1 tsp. **baking soda**
½ tsp. **sea salt**
1 tsp. **cinnamon**
1 tsp. **nutmeg**
1 tsp. pure **vanilla extract**
½ cup **pecans,** chopped
1 cup peeled, grated **apple**

*Makes 36*
*These are more like cakes
than cookies, and are
heavenly warm.*

1. In a large mixing bowl, cream butter thoroughly and add maple syrup in a slow stream.
2. Add pumpkin and egg and mix well.
3. Sift together the flours, baking powder, soda, salt and spices. Stir into butter mixture and add vanilla.
4. Fold in pecans and apple.
5. Spoon by rounded tablespoons onto greased baking pan, leaving 2 inches in between cookies.
6. Bake at 350° for 15 minutes, or until edges just begin to brown.

## Pumpkin Souffle

1 (15 oz.) can **pumpkin**
½ cup **almond milk**
4 T. **butter,** melted
4 **eggs**
⅓ cup pure **maple syrup**
1 tsp. **pumpkin pie spice**
1 tsp. Rumford **baking powder**
¼ tsp. **sea salt**

*Serves 4*

*Good warm or cold.*

*Serve with a little extra maple syrup poured over top if you like.*

1. In a large bowl mix the pumpkin, almond milk and butter.

2. With a wire whisk add eggs, maple syrup, pumpkin pie spice, baking powder and salt.

3. Turn mixture into a buttered 2 qt. casserole.

4. Bake at 350° for 45 - 50 min; until golden brown and a knife inserted in center comes out clean.

## Carob Chip Cookies

1 cup **butter**
¾ cup **honey**
2 **eggs**
1 ½ cups **whole wheat flour**
1 cup **oatmeal**
1 tsp. **baking soda**
½ tsp. **sea salt**
1 cup **unsweetened carob chips**
1 cup **pecans,** chopped
2 tsp. pure **vanilla extract**

1. Cream butter and honey, then add eggs one at a time.

2. Mix flour, oatmeal, soda, and salt. Add to butter mixture.

3. Add chips, pecans and vanilla.

4. Bake on greased baking sheet at 350° 10 min.

## Oatmeal Cookies

---

2 ½ cups uncooked **oatmeal**
1 ½ cups **unbleached white flour**
1 tsp. **cinnamon**
½ tsp. **baking soda**
½ tsp. **sea salt**
1 cup **maple syrup**
¾ cup **butter**
1 tsp. **vanilla**
1 **egg**
½ cup chopped **pecans**

---

1. Combine dry ingredients and mix well.

2. Mix butter, maple syrup and vanilla until smooth. Add egg.

3. Blend in dry ingredients, mixing thoroughly.

4. Stir in nuts and drop by rounded spoonsful onto lightly greased cookie sheet.

5. Bake at 375° approximately 10 min.

6. Cool and enjoy.

## Company Cookies

---

1 cup **butter**
1 cup pure **maple syrup**, at room temperature
2 T. **Pero, Roma** *or* **other powdered coffee substitute**
2 T. **hot water**
2 tsp. pure **vanilla extract**
1 cup **whole wheat flour**
1 ½ cup **unbleached all-purpose flour**

1 cup **pecans,** chopped
1 tsp. **baking soda**
½ tsp. **sea salt**
1 ½ cups **unsweetened carob chips**

---

1. Cream butter well and slowly add maple syrup and vanilla.

2. Dissolve Pero in hot water, add to butter mixture.

3. In a separate bowl toss the flours, pecans, soda and salt. Stir into the creamed mixture.

4. Stir in carob chips. Do not beat. Let batter sit for a few minutes.

5. Drop rounded tablespoons of batter onto greased baking sheet leaving about 2" between cookies.

6. Bake 15 min. at 350°. Transfer to a rack and cool.

## Tootsies

---

½ cup **sunflower seeds,** plain or toasted and salted
½ cup **sesame seeds,** plain or roasted and salted
½ cup **almonds**
½ cup sugar-free **peanut butter, almond butter,** *or* **sunflower butter**
½ cup **carob powder**
½ cup **honey**
½ cup **coconut** *or* **almond flour**
1 tsp. pure **vanilla** *or* **almond extract**

*½ cup unsweetened coconut can be added for a change.*

---

1. Put all in a food processor and process until smooth.

2. Roll and shape into balls or tootsie roll shapes. Refrigerate.

## Peanut Butter Cookies

---

2 ½ cups **unbleached white flour**
1 tsp. **baking soda**
2 tsp. Rumford **baking powder**

½ cup smooth sugar-free **peanut butter**
½ cup extra-light **olive oil**
1 cup **honey**
¼ cup **wheat germ** *or* **bran**
2 **eggs**
2 tsp. pure **vanilla extract**
½ cup chopped roasted **peanuts**
½ tsp. **sea salt**
unsweetened **apple butter**

---

1. In a bowl combine flour, soda and baking powder.

2. In a large bowl, cream peanut butter, oil and honey.

3. Add rest of ingredients in order listed.

4. Mix well and add flour mixture.

5. Drop by rounded tablespoonfuls on an ungreased cookie sheet and bake at 350° 10 - 12 min. or until edges just start to brown.

6. Cool, split cookies and spread with a touch of peanut butter and unsweetened apple butter. Replace top.

## Applesauce Spice Cake

---

½ cup **butter**
¾ cup **honey**
1 **egg**
2 cups **unbleached white flour**
1 tsp. Rumford **baking powder**
½ tsp. **baking soda**
½ tsp. **sea salt**
2 tsp. **cinnamon**
1 tsp. **nutmeg**
½ tsp. **cloves**
1 cup heated unsweetened **applesauce**
½ cup **pecans**, chopped

---

1. Cream butter and honey. Add egg and beat well.

2. Sift a little of the flour over pecans to prevent sinking during baking.

3. Sift rest of flour and dry ingredients.

4. Mix into butter mixture.

5. Add applesauce and pecans, mixing lightly.

6. Pour into buttered 9" square pan and bake at 350° 35 - 40 min.

7. Cool 5 min. in pan, then turn out onto rack to cool completely.

## Baked Apples with Lemon Ginger Sauce

4 **red apples**
juice of 2 **lemons**
½ cup **honey**
1 T. grated fresh **ginger,** peeled and grated **cinnamon**

*Serves 4*

*Good hot or cold.*

1. In a saucepan combine lemon juice and honey. Stir over medium heat until honey is dissolved. Turn off heat and add ginger by grating over saucepan.

2. Core apples and peel top portion only. Place apples in baking dish.

3. Pour sauce over apples and sprinkle with cinnamon.

4. Bake at 350° 30 - 45 minutes until done.

## Apple Pear Crisp

3 **Granny Smith apples,** pared, cored and sliced
3 **Bosc pears,** pared, cored and sliced
¼ cup unsifted **flour,** divided
¼ cup pure **maple syrup**
1 cup crushed **Spelt wheat cereal** (by Arrowhead Mills)
¼ cup **oatmeal**
⅓ cup **pure maple syrup** ⅓ **cup cold butter**

*Serves 4-6*

*You can top the crisp with a sauce made of half almond milk and half maple syrup if you like.*

1 tsp. **cinnamon**
¼ cup chopped **pecans**

---

1.  Butter a 2 qt. casserole. In a bowl mix apples, pears, 2 T. flour and ¼ cup maple syrup. Put in casserole.

2.  In another bowl mix 2 T. flour, Spelt wheat cereal, oatmeal, ⅓ cup maple syrup, butter and cinnamon. Blend with pastry blender. Add pecans.

3.  Sprinkle over apple-pear mixture.

4.  Bake at 375° 40 min.

## Crispy Rice Bars

---

*Add 2 T. unsweetened carob powder to make carob rice bars.*
*Enjoy!*

3 cups crispy **puffed brown rice cereal** *or* **puffed millet**
⅔ cup **peanut butter** *or* **almond butter**—room temperature
⅓ cup **honey**
¼ cup **brown rice syrup**
1 tsp. pure **vanilla**

---

1.  Stir together peanut butter, honey, brown rice syrup, and vanilla in a large bowl.

2.  Add cereal and press into a lightly buttered 8" x 8" baking pan and refrigerate for one hour then cut into bars.

## Carob Brownies

---

1 stick **butter**
6 T. **unsweetened carob powder**
¾ cup **honey**
2 **eggs,** beaten
½ cup **unbleached flour**
¼ tsp. **sea salt**

1 ½ tsp. pure **vanilla** *or* **almond extract**
½ cup **pecans,** chopped

___

1. In a saucepan melt butter with carob powder.
2. Stir in honey and eggs.
3. Sift flour and salt, and add with extract and pecans.
4. Pour into greased 8" x 8" buttered pan.
5. Bake at 350° 30 - 35 min. Cut while warm.

## Pie Crust

1 cup **unbleached white flour**
⅓ cup organic **shortening** *or* organic **coconut oil**
½ tsp. **sea salt**
2 ½ T. **ice water**

___

1. Mix together the flour and salt.
2. Cut in shortening with a pastry blender or knife until shortening is in tiny pieces.
3. Sprinkle on ice water and mix lightly with a fork. Do not knead, but mash into a ball with hands.
4. Roll out on floured surface and place in 9" - 10" pie pan. Press crust down on rim of pan with a fork, and prick crust gently so steam can escape as it browns. Bake at 425° 8 - 10 minutes or until browned

*Makes one crust. Double for double cust.*

*I cook the bottom crusts of all my pies—fruit or otherwise—in order to ensure they are crisp and flaky. Nothing ruins a pie faster than a soggy bottom crust!*

## Carrie's Carob Pie

1 (9") baked **pastry crust** (p. 167)
1 (12 oz.) pk. **unsweetened carob chips**
2 (10 oz.) **Mori-Nu Silken Tofu** (firm), drained

*Serves 8*

½ cup **honey**

2 tsp. pure **almond extract**

---

1. Heat carob chips on low heat just until melted.

2. In a blender or food processor, blend tofu until smooth.

3. Add honey, melted carob chips and almond extract and blend until creamy.

4. Pour filling into baked pie crust and chill thoroughly.

## Cherry Pie

---

*Serves 8*

*This is also delicious poured over shortcake (p. 50) or served alone in parfait glasses.*

1 recipe for **double pastry crust,** (p. 167)

2 (16 oz.) cans **tart cherries** packed in water

¾ - 1 cup **honey**

4 ½ T. **cornstarch**

2 T. **butter**

1 tsp. **sea salt**

1 tsp. pure **almond extract**

---

1. Prepare pastry crust and put half into a 10" pie pan. Bake 8 min. at 425° or until lightly brown. Cool.

2. Drain cherry juice from cans into a saucepan. Add honey, corn starch, butter, salt, and almond extract. Cook until thick and clear, stirring constantly. Remove from heat.

3. Stir in cherries and pour into baked pie shell and top with ventilated or lattice top crust.

4. Bake at 425° for 10 min., then 25 - 35 min. at 375° until golden brown.

## Pumpkin Pie

---

*Serves 6-8*

1 (10") baked and cooled **flour pie crust,** (p. 167)

3 **eggs**

¾ cup **honey**
½ tsp. **ginger**
1 tsp. **cinnamon**
1 tsp. **nutmeg**
½ tsp. **sea salt**
1 ½ cup canned **pumpkin**
1 cup **almond milk**

---

1. Bake pie shell and cool to room temperature.

2. Combine all ingredients in food processor or blender and blend until smooth. Pour into crust.

3. Bake at 425° 10 min. Reduce heat to 350° and bake 35 to 40 min. or until custard is set. Cool.

## Fresh Apple Cake

---

½ cup **butter**
1 cup **honey**
2 **eggs**
2 cups **unbleached white flour**
1 tsp. Rumford **baking powder**
¾ tsp. **baking soda**
1 tsp. **sea salt**
1 tsp. **nutmeg**
1 tsp. **cinnamon**
3 cups pared and chopped **apples**
1 cup **pecans,** chopped

---

*Try peaches when in season for a change.*

1. Cream butter, gradually add honey and beat until light and fluffy.

2. Beat in eggs one at a time.

3. Sift together flour, baking powder, soda, salt, nutmeg, and cinnamon. Gradually add to butter-egg mixture.

4. Stir in apples and nuts.

5. Turn into greased and floured 13" x 9" inch pan. Bake at 325,° 45 min.

## Avocado Ice Cream or Smoothie

*Serves 2*

1 **avocado**
2 tsp. **vanilla extract**
1/3 cup **cashews**
1/3 cup **lime juice**
4 T. **pure maple syrup**
1 1/2 cups **almond, coconut** *or* **hemp milk**

1.  Blend on high until smooth.

2.  Put in freezer for ice cream or drink right away as a smoothie.

## Lemon Coconut Balls

*Makes 15*

*This is an amazing recipe.
All the ingredients are
known anti-cancer and
anti-fungals!
But 2 only please.*

2 cups unsweetened finely shredded organic **coconut,** plus extra
½ cup **almonds**
4 T. organic **honey**
2 T. **coconut oil**
1 tsp. **lemon extract**
**zest** *and* **juice of one lemon**

1.  Place all ingredients in food processor and blend for one minute.

2.  Roll into small balls the size of a quarter.

3.  Roll in extra coconut and place on plate or tray lined in parchment paper. Refrigerate and serve cold.

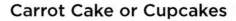

## Carrot Cake or Cupcakes

3 **eggs**
1 cup pure **maple syrup**
½ cup extra-light **olive oil**
1 tsp. pure **vanilla extract**

**grated rind of 1 lemon**
1 ¾ cup grated **carrots**
1 ½ cup **unbleached white** *or* **quinoa flour**
1 cup whole **wheat flour**
1 T. Rumford **baking powder**
½ tsp. **sea salt**
1 tsp. **cinnamon**
½ tsp. **nutmeg**
¼ tsp. **cloves**

———————————————

1.  Beat eggs well and slowly add maple syrup, oil, vanilla and lemon rind. Stir in carrots.

2.  In a large bowl, mix together the flours, baking powder, salt, cinnamon, nutmeg and cloves.

3.  Stir in egg-carrot mixture, blending just until smooth.

4.  Bake at 350° in 9" x 5" greased pan for 50 min. Cool in pan for 5 - 10 min. and turn out onto rack to cool.

*Makes 18*

*I love to make cupcakes with this recipe. Bake at 350\* 15-18 min.*

*Freezes well.*

## What Diet? Ice Cream

———————————————

1 (10 oz.) package of frozen **dark sweet cherries, strawberries, blueberries, raspberries, mangos, mixed berries, etc.**
1 (5.46 oz.) regular canned **coconut milk** (not lite), thoroughly chilled
3 - 4 T. pure **maple syrup**
1 tsp. pure **almond extract, vanilla extract, cinnamon, etc.**

———————————————

1.  Mix all in food processor or blender and serve immediately.

*This is one of my favorite and most versatile desserts. Have fun trying different fruits, spices, and flavorings.*

*Leftovers can be frozen and thawed slightly before serving. My favorite combination is dark sweet cherries, coconut milk, maple syrup and almond extract.*

*Ice cream is easy to adapt to yeast-free cooking. On the following pages are three basic recipes.*

## Carob Ice Cream

*Makes 2 qts.*

*1 cup chopped almonds can be folded in after processing but before freezing.*

2 **eggs**, room temperature
¾ cup **honey**
2 T. **unbleached white flour**
⅛ tsp. **sea salt**
4 cups **almond milk**
4 T. **carob powder**
1 T. pure **almond extract**

1. Beat eggs with mixer until fluffy.

2. In saucepan, combine honey, flour and salt, and gradually stir 2 cups of the almond milk. Cook over medium heat, stirring constantly until mixture coats a wooden spoon, (10 - 15 minutes).

3. To prevent coagulation of the eggs, gradually pour a small amount of the hot mixture into the beaten eggs, stirring with a whisk.

4. Pour egg mixture into remaining hot mixture in saucepan. Cook and stir for 1 min. more.

5. Remove from heat and chill.

6. Stir in remaining 2 cups almond milk and almond extract. Pour into ice cream can and chill until ready to process.

7. Follow manufacturer's directions for processing and freezing.

## Vanilla Ice Cream

2 **eggs**, room temperature
¾ cup **honey**
2 T. **unbleached white flour**
⅛ tsp. **sea salt**
4 cups **vanilla almond milk**
2 tsp. pure **vanilla extract**

1. Beat eggs with mixer until fluffy.

2. In saucepan, combine honey, flour, salt, and gradually stir in 2 cups

of the almond milk. Cook over medium heat, stirring constantly until mixture coats a wooden spoon, (10 - 15 minutes).

3. To prevent coagulation of eggs, gradually pour a small amount of the hot mixture into the beaten eggs, stirring well with a whisk.

4. Pour egg mixture into remaining hot mixture in saucepan. Cook and stir for 1 min. more.

5. Remove from heat and chill.

6. Stir in remaining 2 cups of almond milk and vanilla. Pour mixture into ice cream can and chill until ready to process.

7. Follow manufacturer's directions for processing and freezing.

*Makes 2 qts.*

*Add 2 T. Pero or Roma to hot mixture to make coffee ice cream.*

*Add 5 minutes before end of processing:*
*1 cup unsweetened carob chips to make carob chip ice cream*
*1 cup unsweetened coconut for coconut ice cream*
*2 tsp. cinnamon (no vanilla) for cinnamon ice cream*
*2 cups fresh strawberries for strawberry ice cream.*

## Maple Ice Cream

2 **eggs**, room temperature
1 cup pure **maple syrup**
2 T. **unbleached white flour**
⅛ tsp. **sea salt**
4 cups **almond milk**
1 T. pure **maple extract**

*Makes 2 qts.*

*1 cup chopped pecans or almonds can be folded into mixture after processing but before freezing.*

1. Beat eggs with mixer until fluffy.

2. In saucepan, combine maple syrup, flour and salt, and gradually stir in 2 cups of the almond milk. Cook over medium heat, stirring constantly until mixture coats a wooden spoon, (10 - 15 minutes).

3. To prevent coagulation of the eggs, gradually pour a small amount of the hot mixture into the beaten eggs, stirring with a whisk.

4. Pour egg mixture into the remaining hot mixture in saucepan. Cook and stir for 1 min. more.

5. Remove from heat and chill.

6. Stir in remaining 2 cups of almond milk and maple extract. Pour into ice cream can and chill until ready to process.

7. Follow manufacturer's directions for processing and freezing.

# Baked Pumpkin Custards

*Serves 6*

*Good hot or cold.*

1 ½ cups **almond milk**

4 **eggs**

2 tsp. **pumpkin pie spice**

1 tsp. **cinnamon**

¼ tsp. **sea salt**

¾ cup canned **pumpkin**

½ cup **maple syrup**

1 tsp. **vanilla**

1. Preheat oven to 325°

2. Put almond milk in a saucepan and bring to a simmer. Remove from heat.

3. Whisk eggs, pumpkin pie spice, cinnamon, pumpkin, maple syrup, and salt in a medium bowl. Slowly whisk mixture into warm almond milk,

4. Pour into 6 (4 oz.) ramekins. Set ramekins in large roasting pan and pour warm water to come up half way up the sides of the ramekins.

5. Place pan in oven and bake 50 min., or until knife inserted into center of custard comes our clean.

# Chet's Second Helping Goat Cheese Pudding

2 cups **coconut milk (carton)**

¾ cup **canned coconut milk**

¾ cup **honey**

grated zest of two **lemons**

2 T. **cornstarch**

2 large **eggs**

2 **egg yolks**

1 (10 ½ oz.) log of fresh **goat cheese**

2 T. **butter**

1 T. **lemon juice**

¼ tsp. **sea salt**

1 T. pure **vanilla extract**
**fresh raspberries**

1. In medium saucepan combine coconut milks, honey, and lemon zest. Bring to a simmer, remove from heat, cover and let sit 20 min.
2. In medium bowl whisk eggs with egg yolks and cornstarch until smooth. Gradually whisk into warm milk mixture.
3. Pour into saucepan, bring to a boil over moderately hot heat, whisking constantly until thickened, about one minute.
4. Transfer to food processor, add goat cheese, butter, lemon juice, salt, and vanilla and blend until smooth.
5. Pour into 8 buttered ramekins and refrigerate until cold. Top with fresh raspberries.

*Serves 8*
*(or 7 if Chet is there!).*

*This is one of my top 10 favorite dessert recipes. At a dinner party, our friend Chet finished his pudding and immediately ran into the kitchen hoping to find more. Fortunately I had an extra. He didn't leave the house without the recipe! Don't make it until the third month though.*

## Tonya's Truffles

1 cup **almond butter**
½ cup **butter**
½ cup organic **coconut oil**
¼ cup raw organic **honey**
1 - 2 tsp. **vanilla**
crushed **almonds**

1. Melt all ingredients in a saucepan and mix well.
2. Pour into baking dish and refrigerate four hours until hard.
3. Roll into 1 inch balls and coat with crushed almonds.
4. Keep in refrigerator and serve cold.

*One of my favorite recipes. Every ingredient is a yeast fighter. Serve cold so it won't melt in your hands before it melts in your mouth*

*You can vary this recipe by using peanut butter, using almond extract instead of vanilla, and rolling the balls in finely shredded unsweetened coconut.*

## Faux Fudge

½ cup organic **coconut oil,** melted and cooled
6T. **carob powder**
4T. pure **maple syrup**

*So you miss chocolate?
Try this and you will
actually kill some fungi
since coconut in any form
is an enemy of fungus. Go
easy though…*

2 tsp. pure **almond** *or* **vanilla extract**
½ tsp. **sea salt**

1. Whisk all together and put in a buttered pie plate.
2. Refrigerate or freeze and enjoy.
3. If mixture separates while whisking just chill in refrigerator 20 minutes and stir again.
4. Finely chopped nuts or unsweetened coconut can be added for a change.

## Whipped Cream

1 (5.46 oz.) can **coconut milk,** thoroughly chilled
dash of **stevia** *or* **maple syrup**
pure **vanilla extract** to taste

1. Remove the thick part of the coconut milk and reserve the rest for cooking or smoothies.
2. Whip coconut milk until thick and add the rest.

## Almond Butter Bites

2 cups rolled oats
1 T. ground flax seeds or chia seeds
1/4 cup organic peanut butter
1/2 cup almond butter
1/2 cup raw organic honey
2 Tsp. vanilla
1/2 cup unsweetened carob chips

1. Mix and roll into balls.  Refrigerate.

# Smoothies and Shakes

These are fun and easy to make. Use your imagination. My favorite shake is made with carob almond or rice milk, carob Rice Dream ice cream, a dollop of peanut butter and a couple of drops of almond extract. Worth every calorie! Strawberries, Strawberry Rice Dream Ice Cream and Vanilla Rice Dream are also delish. There is an endless variety of combinations. Enjoy.

## Apple Pie Smoothie

*Serves 1*

1 **apple,** quartered
1 cup **apple juice** (no sugar added, of course)
1 T. **honey**
½ tsp. **cinnamon**
¼ tsp. **vanilla**
1 cup **ice cubes**

1.   Place all in blender and blend on high.

## Blueberry Tofu Smoothie

*Serves 1*

*Good with any berry and most fruits. Great for breakfast. Enjoy!*

½ cup **blueberries**
1 T. **honey**
½ cup **ice**
6 oz. **silken tofu**

1.   Blend until smooth and creamy.

## My Morning Smoothie

*Serves 1*

1 cup **coconut water** *or* **cranberry water** (Knudsen's
cranberry juice diluted 10:1 with water)
1 cup **frozen berries**—
blueberry, raspberry, strawberry, or blackberry
1 T. organic **coconut oil** *or* **high-lignan flax oil**
1 scoop high protein **pea** *or* **hemp protein powder**
1 T. **chia seeds** *or* **almonds**
¼ tsp. **stevia** *or* 1 T. **honey** *or* **maple syrup**

1.   Blend and enjoy.

# Recommended Reading

RECAGING THE BEAST   by Jane Remington

THE FUNGUS LINK I   by Doug A. Kaufmann

THE FUNGUS LINK II   by Doug A. Kaufmann

THE FUNGUS LINK III   by Doug A. Kaufmann

INFECTIOUS DIABETES   by Doug A. Kaufmann

THE GERM THAT CAUSES CANCER   by Doug A. Kaufmann

THE FUNGUS LINK TO HEALTH PROBLEMS   by Doug A. Kaufmann

THE YEAST CONNECTION   by William G. Crook, MD

CHRONIC FATIGUE SYNDROME AND THE YEAST CONNECTION
    by William G. Crook, MD

THE YEAST SYNDROME   by John Parks Trowbridge, MD

CANCER IS A FUNGUS   by Tullio Simoncini, MD

PROOF FOR THE CANCER-FUNGUS CONNECTION
    by James B. Yoseph and Hannah Yoseph, MD

CANCER STEP OUTSIDE THE BOX   by Ty Bollinger

NATURAL STRATEGIES FOR CANCER PATIENTS
    by Russell L. Blaylock, MD

PREVENTION OF BREAST CANCER—HOPE AT LAST—
    by A.V.Costantini, MD

WHAT THE DRUG COMPANIES WON'T TELL YOU AND YOUR DOCTOR DOESN'T KNOW    by Michael T. Murray, ND

VACCINATION VOODOO    by Catherine J. Frompovich

A SHOT IN THE DARK    by Barbara Loe Fisher and Harris Coulter

WHAT YOUR DOCTOR MAY NOT TELL YOU ABOUT CHILDREN'S VACCINES    by Stephanie Cave, MD

REVERSING DIABETES    by Julian Whitaker, MD

THE GREAT CHOLESTEROL MYTH    by Stephen Sinatra, MD

THE CHOLESTEROL MYTHS:  EXPOSING THE FALLACY THAT SATURATED FAT AND CHOLESTEROL CAUSE HEART DISEASE by U. Ravenskov, MD

THE FLUORIDE DECEPTION    by Christopher Bryson

CAFFEINE BLUES    by Stephen Cherniske

SUGAR BLUES    by William Duffy

SWEET DECEPTION    by Joseph Mercola, DO

OVERDO$ED AMERICA    by John Abramson, MD

QUANTUM HEALING    by Deepak Chopra, MD

ALKALYZE OR DIE    by Theodore Baroody, ND., DC

THE pH MIRACLE    by Robert O. Young

WHAT YOUR DOCTOR DIDN'T LEARN IN MEDICAL SCHOOL by Stuart Berger, MD

EXCITOTOXINS THE TASTE THAT KILLS    by Russell Blaylock, MD

YOUR BODY'S MANY CRIES FOR WATER    by F. Batmanghelidj, MD

DOCTORS ARE MORE HARMFUL THAN GERMS by Harvey Bigelsen, MD

VIBRATIONAL MEDICINE    by Richard Gerber, MD

YOU CAN HEAL YOUR LIFE    by Louise L. Hay

THE CURE IS IN THE CUPBOARD    by Cass Ingram, MD

EVIDENCE OF HARM    by David Kirby

HOW TO RAISE A HEALTHY CHILD IN SPITE OF YOUR DOCTOR by Robert Mendelsohn, MD

NONE OF THESE DISEASES    by S.I. McMillen, MD and David E. Stern, MD

DEATH by MEDICINE    by Gary Null

BACK TO HEALTH    by Dennis Remington

*I do hope you will benefit from this important
information for years to come and enjoy
these special recipies prepared with love
over the years for family and friends.*

*I wish you the best of health.*

*Godspeed!*

Jane Remington

Printed in Great Britain
by Amazon